Restoration England

By the same author

1660 The Year of Restoration
Prince Rupert of the Rhine

King Charles II by Sir Peter Lely

PATRICK MORRAH

Restoration England

Constable London

First published in Great Britain 1979
by Constable and Company Limited
10 Orange Street London WC2H 7EG
Copyright © 1979 by Patrick Morrah
Set in Monotype Bell 11 pt
Printed in Great Britain by
Ebenezer Baylis and Son Ltd
The Trinity Press, Worcester, and London

British Library Cataloguing in Publication Data

Morrah, Patrick
  Restoration England.
  1. Great Britain – History – Charles II, 1660-1685
  I.Title
  942.06′6   DA445

  ISBN 0–09–462430–5

Contents

Contents

Illustrations

Preface

Anything approaching a full survey of the Restoration era would demand a book many times the length of this one. What I have attempted here is to build up a picture of what some aspects of life were like in England in the period immediately following the return of King Charles II to claim his heritage after this country's only experiment in republican government.

The years I have chosen run from the restoration of the monarchy in May 1660 to the Fire of London in September 1666, and in recounting public events I have maintained this restriction. In dealing with social and cultural trends, however, it is difficult to keep to so short a period, and I have occasionally strayed outside these limits.

In quoting from seventeenth-century writings I have observed no strict rule on spelling. Where the flavour of the text seemed to demand it I have given the original as it has come down to us; in other circumstances I have modernized. Consistency in the spelling of names is virtually impossible, and I have not attempted it. Intelligibility rather than pedantic accuracy has been my aim. For historical reasons I obstinately adhere to the spelling Stewart in preference to Stuart.

I should like to thank my friends Martin Cooper, Terence Mullaly and Anthony Davey for their help and advice on their specialist subjects; also Mrs E. L. Plant for typing the whole book with an efficiency which I trust will ease the task of the publisher.

Pictures were supplied by Mrs Stuart Rose of Illustration Research Service.

P.M.

The Restoration

All eyes you draw, and with the eyes the heart,
Of your own pomp your self the greatest part:
Loud shouts the Nations happiness proclaim,
And Heav'n this day is feasted with your Name.

John Dryden

On 25 May 1660 King Charles II stepped ashore at Dover from the Admiral's barge of the *Charles* (until recently the *Naseby*), and was received with tremendous enthusiasm by his loyal subjects who had lived, some happily and some with secret loathing, under a republican form of government since the new King's father had died on the scaffold in Whitehall eleven years before. The exile had returned, with the joyful approbation of the country's present leaders, to reclaim the throne that had since been vacant; and he brought with him, in the words of the distinguished historian G. M. Trevelyan, 'the wittiest company of comedians that history records' who 'had come to tread the stage for a while, as little appreciated on the whole by the English people as were the great tragedians who had played their piece and were departing'.

For the moment, at least, England was in the mood for comedy. The era of the Commonwealth and Cromwellian rule had not been conducive to laughter. The Saints who governed the country in a spirit of strict Puritan orthodoxy had many admirable characteristics, but humour and gaiety were not among them. Earnest and fanatical, they waged a relentless war against all forms of frivolity and self-indulgence, curbing the natural instincts of an exuberant and pleasure-loving people with all the legislative weapons that a military dictatorship gave them. The immemorial sports and pastimes of the countryside were controlled, and in many cases suppressed;

Sunday was changed from a carefree holiday to a rigidly regulated sabbath of prayer and penance; Christmas became a
fast-day, and the theatres were closed.

By 1660 England was heartily sick of the rule of the Saints;
and when in the early months of the year it became clear that
the monarchy was on its way back the people of the country
began to make their feelings manifest. Healths were drunk to
Charles II, at first privately and then openly in the streets,
and after the official decision to recall the King, royalist frenzy
took possession of the populace. 'I pray, my Lord,' wrote
Henry Coventry from London to the Marquess of Ormonde on
10 May, 'hasten his Majesty over as soon as may be, to prevent
the town's running mad; for betwixt joy and expectation the
people hardly sleep.'

Thus it was that, on that summer afternoon when King
Charles 'renewed the expiring pomp of May', rejoicing knew
no bounds. Merry crowds flocked into Dover and 'choked up
the beach with their still growing store'; and when the as yet
hardly known monarch set foot on the sands, to be greeted by
the chief architect of the Restoration, General George Monk,
the cheering verged on the hysterical. Charles played his part
to perfection. Tall and graceful, he seemed the personification
of royal dignity. He greeted Monk with affectionate gravity;
and when the Mayor of Dover stepped forward to present him
with a Bible he declared without a trace of irony that it was the
thing he loved above all things in the world. His journey to
Canterbury, first by coach and then, after crossing Barham
Down, on horseback, was a triumphal progress, with joyful
crowds cheering him all the way.

At Canterbury the serious business of the reign, which
nominally had been in existence since 1649, began. Charles
wrote to the Houses of Parliament to give formal notice of
his arrival, received a seemingly endless succession of visitors
and petitioners, and invested General Monk and Admiral
Montagu (who as commander of the fleet had escorted him
home) with the Order of the Garter. On the evening of 26 May

he wrote to his beloved sister Henrietta ('Minette'), who was with her mother in France: 'My head is so prodigiously dazed by the acclamation and by quantities of business that I know not whether I am writing sense or no.'

On the following day, which was Sunday, he proceeded in state to the Cathedral, now restored to Anglican worship but in a sadly shabby condition after years of Puritan neglect and disapproval; and then it was time to plan the culminating event, the ceremonial entry into London. The King spent one night at Rochester, and took the opportunity to inspect his ships at Chatham. Then, at five o'clock on the morning of 29 May, the triumphal cavalcade set out for the capital.

It was on his thirtieth birthday that the King entered London. After reviewing his army at Blackheath he rode in procession between his brothers, the Dukes of York and Gloucester, to the Royal Palace of Whitehall; the streets were thronged, fountains ran claret, ladies watched from every window, bands played and people cheered. It was an exhausting day for the King; he was fourteen hours on the road, mostly on horseback. But his sardonic humour did not desert him. On arriving at Whitehall he remarked that he must have been foolish not to have come home earlier, since every person he had met in England claimed to have always been longing for his return. Then he was glad to get to the bed in the Palace which that night he shared (according to an account which, however, cannot boast contemporary authority) with the reigning royal mistress, Barbara Palmer.

It was all in great contrast with that day, nearly nine years before, when Charles had last left English soil. He had then come over from his exile on the Continent in the hope of restoration; a restoration which had actually taken place in Scotland, of which country he was accepted as King by the ruling Presbyterian clique, being crowned at Scone at the beginning of 1651. But eight months later, advancing into

England at the head of a Scottish army, he was decisively beaten in battle by Oliver Cromwell at Worcester. What followed was perhaps his finest hour. Escaping from the battlefield with a small band of devoted followers, he made his way southwards through England in various disguises, constantly harried by patrolling Cromwellian troops and with a price on his head, hiding in woods and cellars and priests' holes, enduring intense hardship and in daily danger of capture. Through it all he preserved his courage and gaiety which enchanted all who came in contact with him, so that people in all walks of life, notably those in humble circumstances, risked their lives to help him. It was another six weeks before, on 15 October 1651, he was able to escape from Shoreham to France in a small ship whose captain proved loyal. It has been estimated that more than a hundred people recognized him during his flight; not one betrayed him.

In the years that followed the Republican regime took root. At the end of 1653 Cromwell was proclaimed Lord Protector, and for the next five years, with the formidable New Model Army at his back, he ruled as dictator in England. But the root was not deep enough for survival. As is the way with usurpations, Cromwell's depended for its existence on the leadership of the usurper. When his forceful personality was removed by death on 3 September 1658, the constitution he had inaugurated rapidly disintegrated. He had been empowered to name his successor, and in a parody of hereditary kingship he had chosen his elder son Richard. Richard Cromwell, a pleasant and unambitious country gentleman, had neither the will nor the capacity to assert his authority in such difficult times. After a few months he gave up the attempt and retired unobtrusively into private life, leaving the field free for Oliver's surviving generals to struggle for power while the country drifted into chaos and anarchy.

It was now, in the latter months of 1659, that General Monk stepped into the limelight. Monk, a swarthy, somewhat grim-faced Devonian, was one of Oliver Cromwell's most trusted administrators, but he was a comparatively recent Cromwellian. A soldier from his youth, he had fought for Charles I in the Great Civil War until taken prisoner in 1644. Unlike most military men of that epoch he was politically uncommitted. His duty, as he saw it as a soldier, was to support the civil government whatever the complexion of that government might be; and on his release from captivity in 1646, when the royal cause was in eclipse, he had no qualms in giving his allegiance to the Republican authority that had taken the place of the monarchy. Throughout the Protectorate he served as commander-in-chief of the army in Scotland, and was in effect the military governor of the northern kingdom. His administration was a model of efficiency; his troops were well trained, well paid and well disciplined, and in the months following the Protector's death the stability of Scotland presented a strong contrast to the increasing disorder of England.

While the leading generals—Charles Fleetwood, John Desborough and John Lambert—bickered, intrigued and manoeuvred for power, Monk viewed their posturings with a cold and critical eye. All parties, including the Royalists across the English Channel, tried to gain his support; but he committed himself to the support of none, and throughout the summer of 1659 he held his hand.

When he did move, his action was deliberate, decisive, and fully in accordance with his principles. England was without a parliament. The Long Parliament, called in 1640, had been emasculated by Cromwell in 1648, when it had stood in the way of his march to power; and the 'Rump' that remained was sent packing when it in its turn opposed his policies before his assumption of office as Lord Protector five years later. Other parliaments, called at the whim of Oliver and Richard Cromwell, failed to last, and the resurrected Rump, recalled in May 1659, lasted only till October, when it was expelled by force by Lambert.

In these circumstances Monk considered that his intervention was justified. His loyalty was to the civil government, but civil administration had broken down. He declared for the return once more of the Rump, as a preliminary to the restoration of constitutional government; and he prepared to march into England with his army to bring it about. He acted with customary deliberation, purging his forces of untrustworthy officers and making contact with Lord Fairfax, the first Commander-in-Chief of the New Model Army. Fairfax had broken with Oliver Cromwell after the beheading of Charles I, to which he had never consented. Since then he had lived in retirement on his Yorkshire estates. He was one of the greatest magnates in the north of England, and his prestige was unrivalled.

Monk, with a formidable army of 2,000 horse and 5,000 foot, crossed the border on 2 January 1660 and made his way slowly but inexorably towards London. Only Lambert attempted to oppose him in arms, and Lambert's army, ill-paid and ill-disciplined, melted away as soon as the threat appeared. Fairfax had been raising troops in Yorkshire, and he and Monk met in York on 11 January. In London the Rump had once more been recalled, and Sir Arthur Haslerig, a convinced Republican, was the principal leader of what remained of the government. But Monk was in control of the situation, and the Rump did not dare to oppose him. He himself had not at this stage declared for a return of the monarchy. The call was being heard in the country for 'a full and free parliament' and Monk did not oppose it. Meanwhile he made it known that he supported the Rump.

The great march took just a month. On 3 February Monk entered London in triumph with his weather-beaten force intact; his infantry, wrote an eye-witness, 'had the best arms and were the likeliest men that ever I saw'. The capital was in a state of disorder and confusion, and nobody ventured to argue with the victorious general. Henceforth his was the dominant voice in the control of English affairs. On 21 February, at his instigation, the 'secluded members', whom Cromwell had expelled, took their seats in the Commons, and the demand for a full and free parliament was thus fulfilled in the person of the Long Parliament now once more in being. It was nearly twenty years since it had first been called—the famous assembly which had gone to war against Charles I and was now to be instrumental in restoring his son to the throne.

The Long Parliament had in fact never been predominantly in favour of abolishing the monarchy. Left to itself, it might well have come to terms with the King once his forces had been defeated in the field in 1646. But in the all-powerful New Model Army republican feeling had been strong. Hence it was that, in the years that followed, Cromwell had found the Parliament no more amenable to his will than had Charles I. But Cromwell with his military might was able to deal with the members by means that had been impossible to the King. He simply threw them out.

Now, in the early months of 1660, the country moved steadily, and with increasing momentum, towards a Stewart restoration. Royalist enthusiasm became daily more vociferous, and Monk was able, in his shrewd way, to sit back and let public opinion do his work for him, supplying unobtrusive guidance from time to time and lending a helping hand where necessary. Almost from the time of his arrival in London he was receiving Royalist agents in secret, but in public he refrained from committing himself, simply supporting, as a member of the new Council of State, any course which the restored Parliament might take.

In March that Parliament ceased to exist. Long ago, in 1641, it had passed an act laying down that it could not be dissolved without its own consent; and thus, through all the ups and downs of the Commonwealth and Protectorate period, the Long Parliament had legally continued to be England's legislative authority. Now, with the tide of opinion flowing strongly against republicanism, it decided to give that consent in order that a new assembly might be called to decide on the country's constitutional future. Dissolution took place on 16 March. 'We are now at liberty,' wrote Sir Roger Burgoyne, one of the members, 'though much against some of our wills: after many sad pangs and groanes, at last we did expire, and now are in another world.'

The new Parliament—the Convention—met on 25 April. Its temper was overwhelmingly royalist, and there could no longer be any doubt as to the shape of the future constitution. On 1 May England was declared to be a monarchy, and an invitation was sent to King Charles II to resume the throne of his ancestors. The King meanwhile had issued the Declaration of Breda, the manifesto of the Restoration, in which he promised to rule as a constitutional monarch and proclaimed an amnesty for all his subjects who should declare their loyalty 'excepting only such as shall hereafter be excepted by Parliament'.

And so, under the skilful direction of General Monk, events moved on peacefully towards the Restoration. The Proclamation of the royal succession, dating the reign from the death of Charles I, was read in London and Westminster on 1 May, and in other cities and towns on the days following. King Charles and the royal family moved from Breda to The Hague, and the English fleet under Admiral Montagu set forth to meet him at the port of Scheveningen. On 23 May the King and his brothers embarked for their voyage to England.

To observers at the time it seemed a miracle. The change from monarchy to a republic had been made in a welter of blood and agony, with Englishman pitted against Englishman and families split in anger and hate, culminating in the supreme tragedy of the King's death at the hands of a public headsman in Whitehall. Now the change back to monarchy had occurred in joy and sunshine, without bloodshed, without foreign intervention, and with the spontaneous welcome of a united nation. That this had come to pass was due first and foremost to the depth of traditional instinct in the English people, but also to the judgement and statesmanship of General George Monk.

Politically it was a stagnant England to which King Charles returned. Oliver Cromwell's rule had been mainly military, and when, after his death, his generals jockeyed for power while the army disintegrated, the result was a political vacuum. Monk restored some semblance of order to the state, but the time was too short for any constitutional reform. The executive authority was the Council of State, of which Monk was in fact the leader though officially only one of a number of equal members. The Convention Parliament was set up with the one intention of giving legal sanction to the restoration of the monarchy. It did not look beyond the immediate object.

To the returning exiles, however, the form of government under the Republican regime mattered little. Charles II's reign had officially begun in 1649, and nothing enacted since then had any constitutional legality. The whole machinery of state could be swept away and the old forms and the old constitution revived as at the opening of the Civil War. Not that this was an easy task. Reconstruction presented many problems, and the economic condition of the country left much to be desired. There was a vast national debt, and the land question in particular seemed insoluble. There had been whole-sale confiscation of estates under the Commonwealth. Now, naturally, loyal followers of the King expected to have their property restored. But many of these estates had changed hands and were now held by people who had paid good money for them. Simply to hand them back to their pre-revolution owners was manifestly impossible; the problem was to bedevil the restored regime for many years and to lead to countless charges of royal ingratitude.

Obstacles such as this lay in the path of the new monarch and his followers. But in this high summer of 1660 they did not seem insuperable. All that mattered to the people of England was that, after the long winter of Puritan repression, the sun was shining once more on the old life and pleasures of pre-war days, personified in a glittering train of gallant courtiers and lovely ladies such as had graced Whitehall in those happy days before 1642. The King was enjoying his own again.

This King at thirty years of age was a mature, shrewd man of the world, easy-going and cynical, with no illusions in his judgement of human nature. It was his personality, more than any other single factor, that was to shape the coming age; if ever there was a trend-setter, it was he. Just as the Victorian era took its tone from the highly respectable little widow of Windsor, so Restoration England, at least in its fashionable and upper-class aspects, reflected the manners and morals of the witty, good-natured rake who presided over his brilliant and raffish court at Whitehall.

His childhood and youth had been packed with a variety of experience such as is seldom the lot of a monarch in the making. Born on 29 May 1630, he spent his earliest years in the luxurious surroundings of the most cultivated court in Europe. An elder brother, born in the previous year, had lived only for a few hours, and from the beginning the young Duke of Cornwall, as heir to the throne of Great Britain, was the centre of attention, doted on by both his father and his mother. Charles I was a devoted and indulgent parent; a king, moreover, who lived in an atmosphere of stateliness and beauty amid the artistic treasures which it was his delight to assemble in his palaces. The benefits of all this sophisticated elegance, together with the best possible education, were heaped on the destined heir, a singularly strong and healthy child; and though neither intellectual learning nor artistic sensibility proved to be among his more noticeable characteristics, the effects of this cultural upbringing were evident in the poise and ease of manner with which he was able to face the world when the testing time came.

At the age of eight he was declared Prince of Wales by his father, as well as being made a Knight of the Garter; but on account of his youth his installation as Prince was postponed to a future date, and in the event it never took place, owing to the troubles that from this time on took possession of the kingdom that was to be his. The elegant world of Charles I fell to pieces about his ears with growing momentum, and the young Prince found himself, before he had entered his teens, in the midst of a civil war between factions of his future subjects.

The Prince of Wales was twelve when he received his baptism of fire. The first big battle of the war was fought at Edgehill in October 1642, and Prince Charles, with his nine-year-old brother James, was present with the King. When the fighting started the boys were sent to the rear in the charge of no less a person than the great Dr William Harvey, whose name lives in medical history; but in the later stages of the battle a troop of Roundhead horse broke through the Royalist ranks and advanced almost to where Harvey and the princes were standing. Young Charles was in a frenzy of excitement; he brandished his pistol, and crying 'I fear them not!' he rushed to resist the charge. Some Cavalier horsemen appeared; the enemy were diverted and the princes hustled away to safety in a barn. Charles was thwarted in his attempt to strike a personal blow for his father. But he had shown splendid courage, and it was a thrilling moment in his life.

In the next four years he grew up amid blood and arms. He was not again so close to the centre of battle as he had been at Edgehill; but in 1645 he was made nominal General of the West with headquarters at Bristol, the effective commander being his cousin Prince Rupert of the Rhine, the hero of his boyhood. But the fortunes of Charles I were fading fast. If the monarchy was to be saved, it was urgent that the heir to the throne should escape from the country to carry on the fight from abroad. Early in 1646 he left the mainland and took refuge in the Scilly Isles.

It was now that the days of wandering began. In the Scillies the Prince suffered genuine hardship. The weather was severe, and the rain came through the roof of the half-ruined hill-top castle in which Charles and a handful of his father's councillors, of whom the chief was Sir Edward Hyde, took refuge. Fuel was scarce, and it was difficult to keep warm. The little party of exiles subsisted on the small quantities of fish that were available.

After a few weeks they moved on to Jersey, which was still loyal to the Stewart monarchy. Here Prince Charles was received with honour and with acclamation, and here he was able to keep up some semblance of a court. The seven weeks that he spent on the island were among the happiest of his life during the interregnum. He was idolized by the Jersey population, and he amused himself by learning to sail. It may also have been at this time that he began that seemingly endless series of amorous liaisons through which he is best known to posterity, though concrete evidence is lacking. He was sixteen now, and there were some lovely ladies in Jersey. There were stories of an illegitimate son (the first of many) born to him by one of these ladies; and though this alleged affair has been discounted by historians the rumour may well have had some foundation in fact.

But it was time to move on again. Queen Henrietta Maria was in her native France, and she was determined to have her son with her. Hyde, disliking the idea of the heir to the throne being in the hands of a foreign power and fearing for the Prince's Protestant faith under the influence of his Catholic mother, was bitterly opposed to the journey; but the Queen had the support of her husband, now in desperate straits in England, and the young man himself wanted to go. So Henrietta Maria got her way, and at the end of June 1646 Prince Charles joined his mother at her little court at Saint-Germain.

For the next two years his life was aimless and unrewarding. Henrietta was dependent on her French hosts, and her court was chronically short of money. Her brother, King Louis XIII, had died in 1643, and at the time when her son joined her at Saint-Germain the new King, Louis XIV, was eight years old. He was a precocious child, already intensely conscious of his destiny and his royal dignity; but political power was in the hands of Cardinal Mazarin, the close confidant of the Queen Mother and Regent Anne of Austria (some said he was her lover). Mazarin, a supple Italian politician, had been the pupil and protégé of Cardinal Richelieu, that imposing prelate who had been the effective ruler of France throughout most of the reign of Louis XIII. Unlike his predecessor, who in spite of his political preoccupations had held a French bishopric (Luçon) and never entirely neglected his ecclesiastical duties, Mazarin devoted himself exclusively to affairs of state. His status as a cardinal never inspired him to take priest's orders.

Mazarin was concerned exclusively with the advancement of French power. The plight of an exiled English prince was of interest to him only so far as it could be used for diplomatic purposes; and at the moment there was no such opportunity. So Charles was left to kick his heels at Saint-Germain, tolerated but not encouraged by Anne of Austria's French court and kept perennially on short commons.

Plans were of course always being contemplated for improving his fortunes, and Queen Henrietta Maria hoped that he might make an advantageous marriage. The lady chosen was Anne-Marie de Montpensier, Louis XIV's cousin, known to history as 'la Grande Mademoiselle'. She was the daughter of Gaston Duke of Orleans, younger brother of Louis XIII, a prince with a lifelong record of treachery and intrigue; she was haughty, ambitious, eccentric, beautiful and a great heiress. The project was put in hand but it foundered on a simple but formidable obstacle: neither party in the least wanted it to succeed. Mademoiselle had her eye on bigger game than a poverty-striken prince in exile; the Emperor Ferdinand III and King Philip IV of Spain were both possible contenders for the marriage-stakes and, though in the event she won neither, these were the directions in which her eyes were turning. Charles for his part was in no way attracted towards this majestic princess; his inclination was for more accommodating damsels. He made little more than a pretence of wooing, taking refuge in diplomatic inability to make his meaning plain in French; while Mademoiselle, who thought it beneath her dignity to learn so unrefined a tongue as English, treated her incoherent lover with disdain. Charles's cousin, the accomplished linguist Prince Rupert, was called in to act as go-between; but it was all to no avail. Queen Henrietta was compelled to admit defeat.

Prince Charles turned with relief to less awe-inspiring feminine society. A lady in whose company he delighted was the lovely and light-hearted Duchesse de Châtillon, known to him as 'Bablon', one of the gayest ornaments of the French court. There are a number of allusions to her in his letters, and it appears that his attentions to her aroused the anger of Mademoiselle, who, although she had a poor opinion of her reluctant suitor, was not above showing pique and jealousy when he preferred other company to her own. But Bablon, so far as is known, was never the Prince's mistress. Her importance in his life was that her friendship, which he retained for many years, helped to give him self-confidence and proficiency in the arts of the courtier. He came to France a somewhat gauche adolescent, unsure of himself and ill-at-ease in the elegant atmosphere of the highly sophisticated French court. After a year or two in the society of lively and dazzling sirens such as the Duchesse de Châtillon, he was able to mix happily with the lords and ladies of French society on equal terms. At the same time he became imbued with an admiration for the graces of French social life which was to have its effect on the nature of the Restoration scene when he came into his heritage in England.

For the gratification of his fleshly appetites, however, he looked lower than strawberry leaves. Charles's taste in women was catholic, and though details are lacking it is tolerably certain that Nell Gwyn had her French predecessors at this time. Paris in the mid-seventeenth century, as at most periods, was a city where the most elegant social life was counterbalanced by the existence of an extensive underworld of thieves, cut-throats and prostitutes; an underworld little changed from that given immortality in the racy poems of François Villon two centuries earlier. There were plenty of brothels to cater for the pleasures of princes and lesser mortals alike, and Charles, freed now from the influence of his rigid father (his mother, managing woman though she was, could exercise little control over his private life), was able to slip away from court as he pleased and follow his own whims in his leisure hours.

In this side of his life Prince Charles had a boon companion in George Villiers, second Duke of Buckingham, who was two years his senior. Buckingham was the son of King James I's favourite, who had been all-powerful in James's latter years and at the beginning of the reign of Charles I. This Duke was England's evil genius; a man of negligible political capacity and enormous personal extravagance, he had gained his ascendancy through his physical grace and good looks, these characteristics being the quickest way to King James's favour. Once in power he had squandered the nation's money and indulged in reckless policies that brought England to the verge of bankruptcy; among those responsible for the troubles that overtook King Charles he was not the least blameworthy. Yet he was not without a certain nobility of character. He was generous and good-hearted in personal relationships; for the ambitious self-seeker that he was, he was remarkably lacking in malice and vindictiveness. And he had a genuine and cultivated taste in art.

His son, who inherited his flamboyance and his political volatility, was a more complex character. Many years after the Restoration John Dryden summed him up to perfection in his famous satire *Absalom and Achitophel*:

A man so various that he seemed to be
Not one, but all mankind's epitome:
Stiff in opinions, always in the wrong,
Was everything by starts and nothing long;
But, in the course of one revolving moon,
Was chemist, fiddler, statesman and buffoon;

> Then all for women, painting, rhyming, drinking,
> Besides ten thousand freaks that died in thinking.

Buckingham had been an infant when his father was assassinated in 1628. King Charles, heartbroken at the death of his friend, had taken the orphan boy under his wing, together with his brother, the posthumously born Francis, and the two were close companions of the younger Charles throughout their childhood. The young Duke was brilliantly clever, precocious, daring and aggressive; and he acquired an ascendancy over the slower-developing prince which to the end he never quite lost. When the Civil War came George and Francis, boys in their early teens, ran away to take part in the fighting under Prince Rupert, but were whisked away from danger by their guardian, the Earl of Northumberland, and packed off to the Continent to finish their education. In 1646, after an extensive tour of Italy, they joined Prince Charles in Paris.

Buckingham was now eighteen, a self-assured, sophisticated cosmopolitan, witty and unconventional, a brilliant talker ready to pour ridicule on all established values and on staid upholders of the old regime. Prince Charles's official tutor was the philosopher Thomas Hobbes, but it was Buckingham who instructed him in the ways of the world and the seamy side of life, having himself already, in the words of one of his sterner critics, 'got into all the vices and impieties of the age'.

Thus the Prince, exiled and impecunious though he was, managed to amuse himself in Paris if not at Saint-Germain. But while he was completing his education, in more senses than one, things were moving in England. In the summer of 1648 news of great promise reached Saint-Germain. A sizeable portion of the navy had renounced its allegiance to the Parliament and sailed for Holland to put itself at the disposal of the Prince of Wales. Simultaneously a few military garrisons declared for the King, and Royalist risings were inaugurated in various parts of the country. The Second Civil War had begun.

In the event it was an abortive affair, hardly worthy of the name of war; the campaigns at home were quickly settled by Fairfax and Cromwell. But for a time Royalist hopes were high. Prince Charles was thrilled, and delighted to be able to throw off his enforced idleness. He made his way to the Dutch port of Helvoetsluys and there took over titular command of his fleet, at the same time sending for his cousin Rupert to act as his vice-admiral with effective tactical authority. At the same time he did not divorce himself from the new activities which he had found so enjoyable. At The Hague, which became the Royalist headquarters, he became acquainted with a young English exile named Lucy Walter, the first of his mistresses to play a significant part in the history of the reign, if only indirectly. The son she bore him in the following year was in due course created Duke of Monmouth and, during the reign of his uncle James II, came within measurable distance of seizing the English throne.

But Prince Charles did not stay long at The Hague. At Helvoetsluys he took up his command and sailed for England with Rupert in the *Satisfaction*. In the manoeuvres that followed —they were nothing more—he enhanced his martial reputation. The Parliamentarian fleet under the Earl of Warwick was sighted, but no engagement took place. Charles's ships hung about the mouth of the Thames for a month and took a few prizes, but when news came that the Royalist risings had been suppressed the fleet sailed back to Holland. Charles, however, had shown himself a resolute commander. The most serious event in the expedition was a near-mutiny among the seamen in the *Satisfaction*, angry at the paucity of prizes. It was the Prince of Wales, not Prince Rupert, who by his cool courage and firm action quelled the disaffection. He outshone his far more experienced cousin and proved himself capable of commanding at sea.

The next great crisis in his life came with the death of King Charles I. When news reached Holland that the King had been put on trial by his Republican captors, the Prince did everything in his power to save his father's life. He appealed to the courts of Europe, and in particular to the Dutch authorities, imploring them to intercede with the Parliament; and when these appeals failed he sent a blank paper to Westminster, inviting the English rulers to write any terms they chose above his signature if they would only reprieve the King. All was in vain. King Charles was beheaded in Whitehall on 30 January 1649.

The news, broken to the younger Charles at The Hague, affected him as deeply as anything in his life. He burst into tears when he was told, and for a brief period was unapproachable. But he soon recovered his spirits and began to make plans for the future. He was now King Charles II, albeit a monarch in exile, and to his desire to gain the throne of his ancestors was added the incentive of seeking to avenge his father's death. He was now able to exercise an authority which hitherto had been denied him. Declaring Prince Rupert Lord High Admiral —an appointment which only the King could make—he sent him off to Ireland to attempt a landing in that country, and himself prepared to sail for Scotland.

He had already been in touch with the Presbyterian rulers of the northern kingdom, and had been proclaimed King in Edinburgh. But much negotiation was necessary before he could take up his heritage. Scots commissioners visited him at Breda, and after much argument he agreed to sign the Covenant, which established the Presbyterian creed and abjured episcopacy, the cause for which his father had fought to the death. It was here that Charles II first showed the opportunism that became one of his characteristics. He was indeed forced into duplicity. The gallant Marquess of Montrose, the most loyal Scottish supporter of the Stewarts, was planning a new invasion of his country from the Continent, and Charles, in the midst of negotiations with the Marquess's most deadly opponents, created him Governor of Scotland and Lieutenant-General of its forces. He hoped to ensure success by backing both parties. In the event he accepted the Covenanters as the winning side and left Montrose to his fate. His bravest and most brilliant follower was captured by the Presbyterians and suffered the cruellest and most humiliating of deaths on the scaffold. It was the most discreditable episode in Charles II's life.

Once in Scotland, where he arrived in June 1650, the King paid the price of that betrayal. The Scottish regime, dominated by Archibald Campbell, Marquess of Argyll, was of the most rigid puritanical temper. Charles, crowned at Scone on the first day of 1651, found himself treated more like an errant schoolboy than a monarch. He was forced to sign a declaration acknowledging not only his own sins but the sins of his parents and ancestors, compelled to listen to innumerable and interminable sermons denouncing the iniquities of the house of Stewart, forbidden to ride or play games, and subjected to the severest control of the Covenanting ministers. To all these insults and humiliations he submitted with the best grace he could muster, though he was heard to murmur while listening to the catalogue of his sins that he expected next to have to repent of ever having been born.

Seldom, if ever, has a King of England sunk so low. But later in the year 1651 he redeemed himself, to the extent at least of regaining his self-respect if not improving his fortunes. The Covenanters rewarded his grovellings by supplying him with an army, and as commander-in-chief he led it into England. Cromwell was at this time in Scotland with a Roundhead army, having on 3 September 1650 defeated a Covenanter force at Dunbar. When King Charles moved southward, Cromwell followed him; and the two armies met at Worcester on the anniversary of Dunbar. The improvised force of Scots proved no match for Cromwell's trained Ironsides, but they put up a creditable fight and Charles himself showed the utmost gallantry, charging again and again at the head of his troops and having two horses shot under him. Only when the battle was irretrievably lost did he allow himself to be led from the scene of carnage, escaping from Worcester with a handful of loyal companions.

There followed that series of almost incredible adventures of which in later life he loved to talk with growing garrulity.

Adversity brought out the best in his character, and it was his courage and gaiety that above all enabled him, a fugitive prince with a price on his head, to make his way through republican England to the south coast where, in mid-October 1651, he embarked in Captain Tattersall's vessel to return to France. He was once again an exile, but he was freed from Covenant bonds and enriched with new and varied experiences that made him an altogether more mature, self-assured being and prepared him for the years to come.

For the last nine years of his exile King Charles had once more to be content with the role of spectator. He took up his abode in the Louvre in Paris, where his mother had now her court; but France was itself in a state of disorder, and in 1654 he moved to Cologne. In the years that followed he paid a number of visits to other countries, hoping always to find influential backers for his cause. For the most part, however, he left the conduct of political affairs to Hyde and the Marquess of Ormonde, and devoted himself to such pleasures as his chronically impecunious state permitted. His high spirits seldom failed him, and his sunny nature and his optimism at least helped to keep his little court cheerful. He took his pleasures where he could find them and by 1660 it was said that he could boast of having had seventeen mistresses; and doubtless he fathered a few more bastards in this period, though details are lacking.

Eyes were fixed constantly on England, where from time to time Royalist risings were planned and, in one or two cases, took place. But the iron rule of Oliver Cromwell was too firmly established to allow them much chance of success.

Then, in September 1658, Cromwell died. Royalist hopes at once leapt sky-high, and in fact from that time on events moved inexorably towards the return of the monarchy. At the beginning of 1660 Monk began his famous march; in May the final decisions were taken, and on the 29th of that month King Charles entered his capital.

Such were the experiences which had moulded the character of Charles II. Naturally kind, open-hearted and generous, he had seen too much of the malice, duplicity and cupidity of men to retain many illusions where human nature was concerned. His adventures had made him cynical; he did not expect honourable conduct from his fellow-men, and he was prepared to meet them on their own ground. He would lie brazenly when it suited him to do so; he trusted no man and preferred to rely on his own judgement, which was shrewd and penetrating. No man could outwit him; he often gave in to others, but when he did so it was from cold motives of policy and with a view to getting his own way in the end. As for women, the last thing he expected to find in them was chastity, and he was disappointed when he did.

Yet this tall, graceful, charming, humorous man made himself immensely popular among his subjects. He was good-natured and accessible, with an ease of manner that put others at their ease. His wit was proverbial, and he talked brilliantly and interminably. Nobody could doubt his kingliness. While totally devoid of arrogance and enjoying informality, he had a natural dignity whereby he could always maintain his position. And all his vicissitudes had failed to subdue the innate kindliness of his disposition. His policy might be directed by opportunism and cold expediency, but in private life he was the pleasantest and most companionable, the most genial and friendly, of men.

King Charles was far from being an intellectual, as his grandfather James I had been; nor had he the cultivated artistic taste of his father. His brain, however, was of the keenest, and his native curiosity brought him a wide, if not profound, knowledge of men and matters. He profited by experience, and in time became, it might well be said, the most astute politician in his kingdom. His own tastes ran rather to science and practical studies than to art and literature; he had a real knowledge of the technical aspects of shipping and navigation. At the same time he was not unappreciative of those branches of culture to which he did not himself aspire. Artists and scholars found encouragement at his court, and he was an enthusiastic patron of the theatre.

With the King when he landed at Dover were his two younger brothers. James Duke of York, three years his junior, had closely shared his life up to the time of Edgehill, where the two boys had had their first taste of warfare. Later their ways diverged, though not infrequently they were together again. In the final stages of the Civil War James fell into the hands of the Parliamentarians, together with two younger members of the family; but in 1648, at the age of fourteen, he escaped in female garb from St James's Palace, and joined his sister Mary at The Hague. Thereafter he set himself to learn the craft of soldiering. During the interregnum he fought in the armies of both France and Spain, and for four years served on the staff of the great French Marshal de Turenne. With the intensity of his nature he acquired a real knowledge of the military art, rising by his own merit to high rank in the French forces. He was brave and hard-working, and became a thoroughly capable commander, if never perhaps an imaginative leader. Turenne had the highest opinion of his military capacity.

The Duke of York, who was to play an important and influential part in his brother's reign before himself succeeding to the throne as James II, had little in common with his elder brother. They were alike in their addiction to the pleasures of feminine company, but in virtually all other personal characteristics they were as different as two brothers could well be. James had none of Charles's wit or his mental liveliness; nor had he his brother's opportunism or political shrewdness. He was slow-witted, obstinate, and in many ways obtuse. Naturally autocratic, he would pursue his own aims regardless of expediency or the advice of others. In details of practical administration he was highly efficient, and in his principal post of Lord High Admiral he was destined to give splendid service to the Royal Navy.

Of the youngest brother, Henry Duke of Gloucester, there

James, Duke of York, as a young man, by Samuel Cooper. He played an influential role in his brother's reign, before himself succeeding to the throne as James II.

George Monk, first Duke of Albemarle, by Samuel Cooper. Events moved peacefully towards the Restoration under his skilful guidance.

The Coronation and Enthronement of Charles II, from 'The Entertainment of Charles II' by J. Ogilby. *Charles was crowned king in West...*

is little to be said. He was seven years younger than James, and only once had he come into prominence at the exiled court; that was when, in 1654, his mother made a determined effort to convert him to the Catholic faith. Henry, who was then fourteen, had no very strong views on the matter; but his eldest brother, afraid of the effect the conversion might have on his chances of restoration, took vigorous action against the Queen Mother. Henry quickly submitted to his royal brother, and thereafter subsided once more into obscurity. Curiously enough, he was the only one of the three brothers to die a Protestant. He survived the Restoration for less than four months, dying of smallpox in September 1660.

Out of the nine children born to King Charles I and Queen Henrietta Maria, three girls had also survived infancy. None, however, was in England at the moment of restoration. The eldest, Mary, had married Prince William of Orange, Stadtholder of the Netherlands, who had died in 1650. She was now the Princess Dowager, mother of the young William III, born after his father's death. Both she and her husband had done all they could to help her exiled brother, and the English royal family had enjoyed her hospitality at The Hague.

The second sister, the budding bluestocking Elizabeth, was the only intellectual of the family. But her life was short. Captured when Oxford fell to the Roundheads, she was imprisoned with her brothers James and Henry, first in St James's Palace and then, after James's escape, in Carisbrooke Castle in the Isle of Wight, where Elizabeth died at the age of fourteen.

The youngest of the brood, Princess Henrietta Anne, born at Exeter in the later days of the Civil War, when the Queen was on the point of leaving England, was nearly sixteen at the time of the Restoration. She was her mother's close companion, entirely French in her upbringing, and she alone of the family had been raised and educated in the Catholic faith.

Between the eldest and the youngest of the children of Charles I, separated by fourteen years and brought up in

2

different countries, there was a bond of the deepest affection. Princess Henrietta was gay, sprightly, charming, and extremely intelligent. Her brother Charles never knew her till the later years of exile; but then he was enchanted with her. She became his closest confidante, and in the time to come was to play an important part in Anglo-French diplomacy. Charles called her 'Minette', or 'Little Puss', and the love he bore her, undoubtedly the deepest he ever felt for anybody, survives in the many delightful letters he wrote to her.

In affairs of state King Charles, at the time of the Restoration, had three principal advisers—Sir Edward Hyde, James Butler Marquess of Ormonde, and Sir Edward Nicholas. The senior in years was Nicholas. Now in his late sixties, he had been appointed Secretary of State by Charles I before the start of the Civil War, and still held this office under Charles II. He was a man of complete integrity and spotless loyalty. Not unnaturally he looked back to pre-war days as a golden age, and was the most conservative of counsellors.

In personal stature Ormonde was by far the most imposing. Head of one of Ireland's oldest families, he was an aristocrat of aristocrats, combining absolute and unfaltering loyalty with total independence of spirit. He served his royal masters with selfless courage, insisting during the Commonwealth on visiting England in disguise in aid of the royal cause and protesting that he was 'ready to try for a hanging'. Everybody respected him, but nearly everybody stood in awe of him, even Queen Henrietta Maria. When she declared that if she had been properly trusted her son would have been in England, Ormonde replied: 'If it had not been for Your Majesty, he would never have been out of England.'

Ormonde, however, had a comparatively small part to play in Restoration England. His heart was in Ireland, and it was there that throughout a long lifetime he performed his most distinguished services to his King.

The most important of King Charles's political advisers was the Lord Chancellor, Sir Edward Hyde. He was a lawyer-

statesman, fat, pompous, pedantic, and unswervingly loyal. A
Parliament man above all things, he had at the outset of his
career been numbered among the critics of Charles I's policy.
But he was never opposed to the King as such, and when he
saw to what lengths parliamentary opposition was leading he
threw in his lot whole-heartedly with the royal cause. Throughout the Civil War he had stood at the King's side, and since its
end had been firmly attached to the new monarch. He criticized
Charles II's morals, lectured him interminably on his shortcomings in private, but was always ready to defend him in
public. In the future the light-hearted King Charles was to find
him frequently a nuisance, and in the end was to treat him with
ingratitude; but Hyde was the staunchest supporter he had.
Among the upholders of the monarchy in the years following
the Restoration Edward Hyde, Earl of Clarendon as he soon
became, takes the first place.

Sedate figures such as these, however, were not typical of
the new Restoration society as it was destined to develop.
Hyde and Ormonde deplored the company that the King was
tending to keep. For his leisure hours he chose his own companions, and chief among them was the Duke of Buckingham,
who now came into his own. When the royal brothers left
Dover for Canterbury on 25 May 1660, Buckingham went with
them as of right, sitting in the boot of the coach; and thenceforward he was close to the King, the most favoured nobleman
in the land. Another in whose company Charles delighted was
the dramatist Thomas Killigrew, witty and dissolute, who had
led a chequered existence during the interregnum. And there
was Henry Jermyn Earl of St Albans, Henrietta Maria's pet
courtier, who had contrived to keep himself in luxury during
the years of penniless exile. There was Philip Stanhope Earl of
Chesterfield, famous for his proclivity to fighting duels. There
was Charles Sackville Lord Buckhurst, who like Killigrew
combined literary activities with the wild life of a dissipated
courtier and man-about-town. Buckhurst was an elegant poet
of considerable talent; on the other hand, in the early years of

the Restoration, he would be in trouble with the authorities as a murder suspect. He was twenty-two years old at the time of King Charles's return, and was soon renowned for debaucheries which hovered on the line between blackguardism and crime.

A boon companion of Buckhurst was Sir Charles Sedley. Like his friend he was a talented poet, and was soon to make a reputation as a dramatist; and he joined in many of Buckhurst's wilder frolics. Indeed it is difficult to draw much of a distinction between these two brilliant and dissipated young men. They were ornaments of the literary scene, and they were responsible for much of the licentious reputation of the Caroline court. Charles II delighted in the company of both of them.

There were many others of a similar kind. King Charles was already a rake, and he liked to have rakes around him. What can be said of his favourite companions is that a good proportion of them could boast the redeeming features of wit and literary capacity.

Then of course there were the ladies. Lucy Walter had been pensioned off, and now, after some years of increasing misfortune, had died. But there were plenty of charmers eager to catch the royal eye, first and foremost among them being Barbara Palmer. Born Barbara Villiers, daughter of the Royalist soldier Lord Grandison, she was related to Buckingham. At the time of the Restoration she was nineteen years old and had already become known as the mistress of Lord Chesterfield. She had recently married Roger Palmer, a young lawyer of good family and a complaisant cuckold. Where and how King Charles first met her is not known, but certainly their love affair had developed on the Continent before the return to England. Whether or not he slept with her on that first night of his entry into London, she was soon established in Whitehall. Before long she had become the nearest equivalent yet known in England to the *maîtresse en titre* who was accustomed to occupy an almost official position at the court of the King of France.

These and others like them were the merry souls who made up the 'wittiest company of comedians that history records'. They were to set the pattern for the age that was to come.

Court and Country

Though for a time we see White-Hall,
With cobwebs hanging on the wall,
In stead of silk and silver brave,
Which formerly it used to have;
  With rich perfume in every room,
  Delightful to that Princely Train:
Which again you shall see, when the time it shall be,
  That the King enjoys his own again.

Martin Parker

King Charles and his princely train, as we have seen, returned to England in a blaze of glory, with fountains running wine in the streets of London, citizens drinking the loyal toast on their knees, bonfires burning along the length and breadth of the country, and everywhere British subjects letting themselves go in an orgy of joy. Superficially at least there were all the signs of a population rejoicing in the sudden release from the repressions of Puritanism and a return to the half-remembered glories of the old regime.

It is easy, however, to exaggerate the change that took place in the minds of men and in the life of the people. We have seen similar manifestations in our own time. Armistice Day in 1918, and in a lesser degree V-E Day in 1945, echoed the spirit of 1660; and these celebrations did indeed coincide with a real change in the fundamentals of national existence. Talleyrand is said to have remarked that those who had not lived before 1789 did not know how pleasant life could be, and much the same could perhaps be said of 1914 and 1939. At least it can be taken as true that for the vast majority of the people of Britain conditions could never be the same after as before either World War. For good or evil a way of life had gone which could never be replaced.

But the seventeenth century was very different from the twentieth. In that age of slow travel, sluggish communication, unsophisticated administration and a largely illiterate population, it was far harder for events to impinge on public consciousness. The influence of the most forceful of rulers was severely limited. Neither a dictatorial monarch nor a republican enthusiast could shape the lives of those subject to him, even had he wished to do so, as did Hitler and his storm-troopers 300 years later. England might be engulfed by civil war, but the effects of that war were felt, in the main, only where the armies marched or the tax-gatherers were able to penetrate. Below the level of strife and oppression the people of England carried on their lives as they had done from time immemorial, working and suffering, tilling the ground for a bare living, eating well in good times and sometimes starving in bad, drinking and copulating at all times, quarrelling with their lords and masters and bickering with each other, in much the same routine of life as their ancestors had followed for centuries regardless of the warnings and posturings of remote beings who disputed the government of the country. To suggest that in the period 1640–1670 there were communities whose members never heard of Charles I, Cromwell or Charles II would perhaps be an exaggeration; but it is not beyond the bounds of possibility.

Sometimes, in places where war penetrated, conditions became intolerable; and occasionally the sufferers rose in wrath. This happened in the West Country in the early months of 1645. Years of military exactions, of billeting of troops and soldiers 'living off the country', led to a rising of 'clubmen' who attacked both sides indiscriminately, armed with agricultural implements and whatever rustic weapons they could raise. For some months they added materially to the problems faced by the military leaders (principally the Royalists, who were in the ascendancy in the West at that time). But the clubmen were suppressed and were heard of no more.

Yet the civil wars and their aftermath did make a considerable impression in the country at large. The Puritans were
zealous enough in their efforts to change the life of the people,
and to a limited extent they succeeded. Country pleasures
were subjected to vigorous supervision; games were suppressed,
sexual morals strictly scrutinized. The days of thought-police
were far in the future, but the Saints of the 1650s exercised
what control they could over the private lives of ordinary
people.

Their aim was not a classless society; only a few enthusiasts,
such as the Levellers, had any such vision. But in some parts
of England at least there does seem to have arisen the tendency,
familiar in other ages of revolution, to cultivate an appearance
of 'proletarian' drabness and to show resentment at any
display of prosperity. A passage in the memoirs of the Yorkshire squire Sir George Reresby is revealing. Reresby was a
minor in the war years, and subsequently, uneasy in the
atmosphere of the new regime, spent most of his time travelling
on the Continent; but in 1658 he returned to England and
paid a visit to the capital.

> The citizens and common people of London [he recorded]
> had then so far imbibed the customs and manners of a
> Commonwealth, that they could scarce endure the sight of a
> gentleman, so that the common salutation to a man well
> dressed was 'French dog', or the like. Walking one day in
> the street with my valet de chambre, who did wear a feather
> in his hat, some workmen that were mending the street
> abused him and threw sand upon his clothes; at which he
> drew his sword, thinking to follow the custom of France
> in the like cases. This made the rabble fall upon him and me,
> who had drawn too in his defence, till we got shelter in a
> house, not without injury to our bravery and some blows
> to ourselves.

London, however, was not England. On his estate at Thrybergh

Reresby lived much as his ancestors had done, without trouble from the lower orders. Prejudice against wealth and prosperity does not seem to have penetrated far into the countryside. Cromwell's ideal of a community based on the distinction between nobleman, gentleman and yeoman was generally accepted. The squire was respected as he had always been.

In contemplating the social life of the English people as a whole it is fair to conclude that changes in conditions from the beginning to the end of the seventeenth century were less far-reaching than those in the period between 1914 and 1945.

This said, it may also be granted that the 1640–1660 era, when the great issue of the respective powers of King and Parliament was thrashed out (though not finally), first on the battlefield and then at the seat of government, saw the biggest social upheaval in England since the dissolution of the monasteries in the early sixteenth century. And it was in 1660 that the issue, for the moment at least, seemed settled. The year, therefore, was a real landmark.

Such change as did come over England at the Restoration was felt mainly in London, and at the top. First and foremost there was the presence once more of a royal court: a court moreover with essential differences from any which had been known in the country before. Kingship in England, as in other countries, had grown up over the centuries with its own traditions. In the earliest days the monarch was the man best qualified to lead his followers in battle, the strong man most capable of protecting the people subject to him against the foes always in evidence in primitive times. As such he was entrusted with special privileges to give him strength and his rule stability. Above all the hereditary principle was invoked, so that the regime once established could be perpetuated and a peaceful succession ensured when a ruler died; the danger of civil strife, weakening internal security in the face of menace from without, could thus be minimized. The case for hereditary monarchy was admirably put in the period now under discussion by John Dryden, who spoke of our ancestors:

Who, to destroy the seeds of Civil War,
Inherent right in Monarchs did declare:
And, that a lawfull Pow'r might never cease,
Secur'd Succession, to secure our Peace.

A typical king of the primitive type was Alfred the Great,
arguably the most brilliant individual who has ever occupied
a British throne. We know little or nothing of the nature of
Alfred's court, if such a thing can really be said to have existed.
He was almost constantly at war, fighting here, there and
everywhere against the deadly Danish invaders who threatened
to engulf his kingdom, though remarkably he found time in
the intervals to lay down new laws and bring education and
culture to his rude Saxon subjects, to watch over ecclesiastical
appointments and control the administration of the native
church, and himself to translate Latin works for the benefit
of his largely illiterate priesthood. He kept up a continually
moving military headquarters rather than a court; but it was
this that set the pattern for the future. Alfred was the real
founder of the British hereditary monarchy, and his direct
descendant reigns at Westminster today.

As his successors consolidated their power and influence,
always keeping the glorious example of Alfred in mind,
English kingship subtly altered in nature. With the extension
and development of medieval Christendom, the all-pervasive
Catholic Church imparted its blessing to the kingly office,
and with the sacred rites of coronation and anointment conferred
a mystical character on its holder. The King was no longer
merely a leader in battle and council, *primus inter pares* among
his generals and ministers, but an exalted being whose anointed
hand it was a sacred privilege to kiss, a being on whom
God had conferred a peculiar character, *persona mixta* as the
jurists called it, the character of a person half-priest, half-
layman.

Thus through the Middle Ages the aura surrounding
royalty developed to a degree undreamed of in the days of

Alfred and his European contemporaries. A Saxon sovereign indeed received profound respect from his subjects; but it was a respect conferred primarily by his power to protect them against enemies internal and external, the respect felt by loyal soldiers for their general. Now the King was venerated for the sacred nature of his holy office; he might be a minor, even an infant, but wherever he went he was surrounded by bowing courtiers who addressed him on bended knee. To oppose him was as much blasphemy as treason. This concept was put by Shakespeare into the mouth of Richard II, in whose brief years of absolute power the mystique of medieval royalty reached its apogee:

Not all the water in the rough rude sea
Can wash the balm from an anointed king;
The breath of worldly men cannot depose
The deputy elected by the Lord.
For every man that Bolingbroke hath press'd
To lift shrewd steel against our golden crown,
God for his Richard hath in heavenly pay
A glorious angel; then, if angels fight,
Weak men must fall, for heaven still guards the right.

And so with the passing of the centuries the royal court took on the nature of a temple, with courtiers and priests and laymen combined in worship of the monarch. And inevitably a host of ceremonies grew up to regulate the worship. A subject must not turn his back on his sovereign; he must stand while that sovereign sat to take his meals; he must not address him unless spoken to first. Such was the origin of the elaborate ritual of court etiquette.

At the same time it must be emphasized that king-worship in England and in Western Europe never reached the extent of subservience known in eastern countries and in such semi-oriental states as Russia. The King might in theory be a semi-divine being, but there were always nobles who knew the extent of their own power and, however abjectly they might perform their royal duties at court, were ready whenever it suited them to defy their sovereign in their own interests, in arms if need be. Absolute royal power was foreign to English and feudal tradition. When Richard II attempted it he was quickly overthrown.

The essential point about the English court, however, is that virtually to the end of the Middle Ages it remained peripatetic. The King might have his particular palace at Westminster, but he took the court with him wherever he happened to be. And though his role as a military commander gradually declined he was still compelled, in order to keep control of his scattered and isolated domains, to be almost continually on tour; royal 'progresses' were an essential element of the constitution. There was also a more mundane reason for progresses. In days of primitive sanitation a building occupied by a large concourse of people sooner or later became uninhabitable; it was necessary to move on somewhere else and give time for it to be cleansed.

It was under the Tudors that the court assumed the character which, subject to the inevitable changes of time, it still bears. It did not become static; it has never been that. But it moved within a recognized range of royal palaces centred on, and within reasonably easy distance of, the seat of administration at Westminster. The sovereign might still impose the grace of his or her presence on the hospitality of some wealthy subject (sometimes to that subject's financial near-ruin, which he might think a fair price to pay for the privilege of basking in the royal eye), but the place of majesty became fixed in a restricted and predictable orbit. There thus grew up an order of permanent courtiers, akin to the parallel order of civil servants and quite distinct from the magnates of the countryside, whose lives revolved around the person of the monarch and who themselves formed the élite of the country, 'the glass of fashion and the mould of form', in which the social life of the upper classes was reflected.

The court of the Tudors was more gorgeous and colourful than anything of the kind that England had seen before. Henry VII was too busy, too frugal, and too intent on consolidating his position and defending his dubious right to the throne to pay much attention to establishing a court. But he played his part to the extent of bringing the great families to heel, impoverished and enfeebled as they were by the civil wars of the fifteenth century, and inducing them to seek their fortunes rather through royal favour than by independence of the crown. Just as monarchical power came to fruition under the Tudors, so social life became centred in the physical presence of the monarch. The scene might be at different times St James's Palace, Windsor Castle, Richmond, Greenwich or Nonsuch; it was the same scene, and the world of fashion took dictation from the aristocrats assembled there.

Henry VIII, in contrast to his austere father, was a glittering social figure. He saw himself as the complete man on the Renaissance model: soldier, statesman, aesthete, musician, scholar. His court was thronged by leaders of thought and action, artists and men of letters, from all over Europe. His entertainments were of the most lavish description, his ceremonies more splendid and elaborate than anything that could be seen abroad. When he crossed the Channel in 1520, taking the cream of his entourage with him, he and his Renaissance rival Francis I of France provided the most magnificent spectacle of the century at the Field of Cloth of Gold. And it all centred in the King.

The next two reigns were short and troubled, and social life took a back seat. But under Elizabeth I the court took on new glories. With a woman on the throne, and one who loved flattery and ceremonious adulation, young men of pride and ambition vied with each other in paying court to a sovereign who revelled in their obsequious attentions and in distributing her favours among them with caprice. Led by such glittering figures as Robert Dudley Earl of Leicester, Sir Walter Raleigh, and Robert Devereux Earl of Essex, the court became more splendid than ever, and its ceremonies more sophisticated and elaborate.

With the accession of the Stewart dynasty there was a change, though it was not immediately apparent. James VI had been King of Scotland almost from birth, so when he became James I of England at the age of thirty-six he was an experienced sovereign who had presided over his own court for as long as he could remember. This idiosyncratic monarch was as determined as his predecessor had been to exact respect from those beneath him, but he brought with him the manners of a ruder, more unruly society than that of the southern kingdom. Ceremony under James I was as ornate as under Elizabeth, possibly more so. But a rowdiness and looseness of behaviour, such as the great Queen would never have tolerated, came to be accepted.

There was also the matter of the new King's unconventional sexual aberrations. Elizabeth had had her favourites and sycophants. James had his, but unfortunately they belonged to his own sex. The King made no secret of his predilections, and the recipients of his favours responded accordingly. James I was a lavish spender; his court was magnificent in its be-jewelled splendour. But the common sight of a drunken king mauling and caressing his male minions did not add to its dignity.

As the reign moved on these tendencies became more evident, and the magnificence of the court was marred by an increasing sleaziness. Sir John Harington's famous description of the entertainment put on for James's brother-in-law Christian IV of Denmark has been often quoted but will bear repetition:

One day, a great feast was held, and, after dinner, the representation of Solomon his Temple and the coming of the Queen of Sheba was made, or (as I may better say) was meant to have been made, before their Majesties, by device of the Earl of Salisbury and others.—But, alas! as all earthly things do fail to poor mortals in enjoyment, so did prove our presentment hereof. The Lady who did play the Queens part, did carry most precious gifts to both their Majesties; but, forgetting the steps arising to the canopy, overset her caskets into his Danish Majesties lap, and fell at his feet, tho I rather think it was in his face. Much was the hurry and confusion; cloths and napkins were at hand, to make all clean. His Majesty then got up and would dance with the Queen of Sheba; but he fell down and humbled himself before her, and was carried to an inner chamber and laid on a bed of state; which was not a little defiled with the presents of the Queen which had been bestowed on his garments; such as wine, cream, jelly, beverage, cakes, spices, and other good matters. The entertainment and show went forward, and most of the presenters went backward, or fell down; wine did so occupy their upper chambers. Now did appear, in rich dress, Hope, Faith, and Charity: Hope did assay to speak, but wine rendered her endeavours so feeble that she withdrew, and hoped the King would excuse her brevity: Faith was then all alone, for I am certain she was not joined with good works, and left the court in a staggering condition: Charity came to the King's feet, and seemed to cover the multitude of sins her sisters had committed; in some sort she made obeisance and brought gifts, but said she would return home again, as there was no gift which Heaven had not already given his Majesty. She then returned to Hope and Faith, who were both sick and spewing in the lower hall. Next came Victory, in bright armour, and presented a rich sword to the King, who did not accept it, but put it by with his hand; and, by a strange medley of versification, did endeavour to make suit to the King. But Victory did not triumph long; for, after much lamentable utterance, she was led away like a silly captive, and laid to sleep in the outer steps of the anti-chamber. Now did Peace make entry, and strive to get foremost to the King; but I grieve to tell how great wrath she did discover unto those of her attendance; and, much contrary to her semblance, most rudely made

war with her olive branch, and laid on the pates of those who
did oppose her coming.

Such was the standard of conviviality found acceptable at the
court of James I; though one must allow for the pardonable
exaggeration of a public servant who looked back with nostalgia
to the more decorous days of Elizabeth. Nor should one forget
that more elevated entertainments also had their place. It was
in this reign that the court masque came into its own. James
was a highly intellectual monarch, and he availed himself of
the services of the most scholarly of poets, Ben Jonson, to
write words for these elaborate spectacles; and with the settings
designed by Inigo Jones, who held the post of Surveyor to
the Crown, they attained the highest degree of intellectual and
aesthetic excellence. The Queen, Anne of Denmark, delighted
to act in them, to the scandal of the increasingly vocal puritan
opposition to whom the appearance of a female on any sort of
stage was anathema.

The accession of Charles I in 1625 saw great changes in
court life. Gone was the grossness that had characterized his
father's rule; gone too was much of the intellectual element,
for Charles, a man of exquisite taste in the visual arts, was not
greatly attracted towards literature or scholarship. The masques
went on, and became musically and artistically more elegant
than ever under the presiding genius of Inigo Jones; and Queen
Henrietta Maria took up the role of her mother-in-law. But
the ageing Ben Jonson fell into disfavour.

In general the contrast between the courts of the first two
Stewart sovereigns could hardly have been greater. Charles I
was grave, earnest, and intensely virtuous. He was also aloof
and reserved; formality was an integral part of his personality.
He had been a devoted son, but the bawdiness and ribaldry
that characterized his father and his father's circle were foreign
to his nature. Under his rule the court became more elaborate
than ever, with every individual playing his or her prescribed
part with formal precision. Drunkenness was outlawed; only

the most conventional behaviour was permitted in the presence of the King.

At the same time, while the court of Charles I became perhaps the most formal in Europe, it was also the most cultivated. The King was a figure of superb dignity, and dignity and grace were the most noticeable features of the society in which he moved. His taste was impeccable, and some of the finest artists in Europe made their way to his court. Rubens and Van Dyck both enjoyed his patronage and his employment, while among native artists William Dobson was engaged as a court painter. The King built up one of the finest royal collections of pictures ever known, unfortunately to be dispersed during the troubles that followed his reign; and the first Duke of Buckingham, the disastrous royal favourite who was at the same time a discriminating connoisseur of the arts, was commissioned to buy for his master the finest masterpieces that could be obtained.

All this splendour came to an abrupt end at the beginning of 1642 when King Charles, yielding to pressure from his rebellious subjects, left Westminster with his family, to return only in the last weeks of his life when he was brought as a prisoner to St James's Palace before meeting his death at Whitehall.

The royal court ceased to exist. Whitehall Palace, the status of which as the King's principal residence had been consolidated in the first half of the seventeenth century, was used by the Republican authorities as an administrative head-quarters rather than a centre of fashion and ceremony. The palace itself was neglected, 'with cobwebs hanging on the wall'; there was no place for fripperies in the dour regime of the interregnum. Nor was there any perceptible change when Cromwell assumed quasi-royal power as Lord Protector in 1653. He used Whitehall as his residence but eschewed all regal state. No courtier from the luscious days of James and Charles could feel at home in the Protectorial atmosphere of the 1650s.

So when Charles II returned to Whitehall and set up his own court he was able, in such matters as he wished, to start from scratch. Only to a limited extent did he do so. His aim was, naturally, to restore the dignity and splendour that he remembered from those happy days of his childhood before blood and destruction had overwhelmed his father's regime. But what has been destroyed can never be completely rebuilt in its old form, and in some ways this was an advantage to the new sovereign. He was able to restore what he admired and abandon what he did not, without being hampered by the restrictions of a continuous tradition.

Ceremony still ruled the court, and this accorded fully with the King's own desires. But much of the gravity and formalism so dear to the heart of Charles I was dropped, without a return to the vulgarity and excesses associated with King James. Court life as developed by Charles II was influenced by two principal elements: his own temperament and his continental experiences. James I as King of Scotland had paid one visit to Norway, when in an uncharacteristic gesture he had gone to rescue and fetch home his intended bride who was storm-bound on the coast. His son, as Prince of Wales, had indulged in a rather ridiculous expedition to Spain to woo the Spanish King's sister. Apart from these two journeys, both taking place before their accessions to the English throne and both somewhat oddly connected with affairs of the heart, neither monarch had ever left Great Britain. But Charles II was a cosmopolitan. His formative years had been spent in various countries; sometimes fêted and sometimes on the run, he had learned more about life in foreign lands than any English sovereign since the Middle Ages.

Above all he had seen at close range the most splendid and sophisticated court of all, that of Louis XIV of France. Louis had been a monarch since the age of five, but his early years had been spent in a turbulent atmosphere of political instability, intrigue and civil war. From these troubled years he had emerged as a shrewd young man of strong character who knew exactly what he wanted and how to set about getting it. His first object was to subdue the ambitions of the powerful French nobles whose independence of spirit had kept the crown in a state of insecurity, particularly in the anarchic years that followed the deaths of Louis XIII and Richelieu. Louis XIV's solution of the problem was to take the nobles off their estates, where they exercised almost sovereign authority, and bring them to court where he could keep an eye on them and provide them with ceremonial sinecures to keep them happy.

To achieve this object he set about creating a court of such magnificence that his most illustrious subjects could feel it an honour and a pleasure to dance attendance on their awe-inspiring sovereign and bask in the glory of his presence.

At the time of the English Restoration King Louis was twenty-one years old, in the first flush of his determination to make himself the central figure of European civilization—the 'Sun-King' who would in due course create at Versailles the perfect example of a royal court. There, where his father had kept a small country seat in which to find relief from the cares of government in Paris, he would build a palace to eclipse the most grandiose dreams of Habsburg and Romanov, a centre of courtliness and culture which would dictate the fashions of the world and provide a haven and inspiration for poets, painters and musicians.

For literature and art were as important as ceremony at the court of the Sun-King. Louis was a man of genuine and discerning taste, and he wanted the best of everything. Culture certainly took second place to rank, and it would be an exaggeration to say that writers, artists and musicians met aristocrats at the Louvre on equal terms; but they had their place there none the less, and it was not a humble one. Molière, Bernini and Lully were among many of their kind who owed much of their fame and prosperity to the patronage of King Louis.

It was, however, the stateliness of the French court that

above all distinguished it. The Spanish court of Philip IV was equally formal, perhaps more so; but it was less tidy, less marked by *politesse*. At the Louvre in Paris, and later at Versailles, everything down to the last detail was regulated by etiquette; every man and woman knew his or her own place, and the whole elaborate machinery moved with the ease of perfect management. The rigid formality certainly made life excruciatingly dull for those of the courtiers who hankered after more lively pleasures; but life at the top under Louis XIV had a grace and dignity that no other court could boast.

It was the dignity and the culture, the courtliness, that appealed to the English exile. Charles II was not an intellectual like his grandfather, nor a connoisseur of art on the scale of his father; but he, like his cousin Louis, was a man of taste. He liked to have grace and beauty around him (particularly the beauty of women), and as far as elegance and dignity went he modelled his court on that of France. French art, French music, French fashions, pervaded the high society of Restoration England; also French cooking and French wines. 'Everything new came from Paris,' Sir Arthur Bryant has written, 'the Mecca of the civilized world, from sedan chairs and dainty silver brushes for cleaning the teeth to Chatelin's famous fricassees and ragouts.' King Charles moved happily and easily among his foreign protégés, while his own wit and sparkling conversational powers set the tone of a cultural court.

At the same time the court of Charles II was no slavish imitation of that of Louis XIV. The excessive formality of the latter was not copied. Charles was the most approachable of monarchs, and he tempered the ceremonial ritual of court life with an informality all his own. He had the truly royal quality of being able to relax with all and sundry without sacrificing his own regal dignity. Louis had that same quality, but in a different degree. The French King was renowned for his courtesy and affability in conversation with his subjects, but the element of awe was always in evidence; there was a remoteness and a consciousness of his royal isolation which could never for a moment be forgotten. Charles would talk and joke with whoever might catch his ear with a familiar geniality that seemed to take no account of his position. His natural dignity eliminated any need to underline his royal status. The court of Whitehall, taking its cue from its source and fountain, thus took on an air of gaiety and informality in strong contrast with its Parisian counterpart.

In no aspect of life was the change more apparent than in dress. The Puritans had looked askance at sartorial exuberance, and costume under the Commonwealth was distinguished only by its drabness. As always, there were exceptions. General Lambert, most dynamic of Cromwell's lieutenants, was renowned for his elegance, while some lovely ladies defied the conventions of republican fashion so far as they could; it takes more than official disapproval to deter a woman of taste and beauty from striving to look her best. But fashion takes its cue from the top, and the Lord Protector and his family could by no stretch of the imagination be called patterns of elegance. Bluntness of speech and plainness of dress characterized the Cromwell circle; and the populace followed its example.

Then came King Charles II with his train of dandies and cocottes, displaying in dazzling colour the fashions of the French court; and the stay-at-home English, tired of the dullness of the interregnum, joyously imitated them so far as their means allowed. A gentleman of the Restoration was a splendid sight in his flowered coat and doublet, worn over a shirt of ruffled lawn, with lace bands and cuffs falling over his wrists. An embroidered waistcoat hung low over close-fitting breeches beribboned at the knee, above stockings of silk and elaborately buckled shoes. On his head he wore a voluminous curled periwig, a new Paris fashion which replaced the long hair of the earlier part of the century, and over the wig was a low-crowned beaver hat wreathed with feathers. At his waist hung a sword with ornamental hilt and sheath.

Feminine fashions, as always, were even more ornate, with a frankly erotic appeal that appalled the more austere survivors from the previous age. A wasp-waisted bodice was worn with an almost square *décolletage*, seemingly on the point of sliding off the shoulders and keeping the opposite sex in perpetual hope that the operation would be completed. The flowing skirt gave provocative glimpses of the under-petticoat which, previously utilitarian, at this period took on a seductive significance: Herrick's 'winning wave (deserving note) in the tempestuous petticoat'.

Wigs were not unknown among the ladies; but in general women got the effects they wanted from the elaborate and exotic display of their own hair, curled over the forehead, arranged with a dazzling array of coloured ribbons, and flowing luxuriously over the shoulders.

The increasingly erotic note in fashions of dress played its part—either as cause or effect, perhaps something of both— in the best-known aspect of Charles II's court, the looseness of sexual morals. That court has become a byword for lasciviousness and the predominance of abandoned women, partly owing to the fulminations of puritan-minded critics and partly to King Charles's own reputation as a libertine and as a seducer. Actually high society in Restoration England was no more profligate than at most royal courts in most periods; there was as much womanizing at the Louvre (and perhaps at the Vatican) as there ever was at Whitehall. But certainly at this palace it was openly practised for all to see. In this, as in most things, exalted subjects took their cue from the King, who flaunted his mistresses with joyous abandon and cynical disregard for the opinions of the more austere. The solemn John Evelyn, as loyal a Royalist as one could find, was often shocked by what he saw; and even the more down-to-earth Samuel Pepys sometimes recorded the shameless behaviour of his social superiors with awed and secretly fascinated disapproval.

It must not be forgotten that royal mistresses were a phenomenon new to even the oldest of English observers. Charles I had been a model of chastity; his father James, with all the bawdiness of his court, had been uninterested in heterosexual activity. Before the Stewart regime there had been two queens and a boy king on the throne. So it was not since the far-off days of Henry VIII that there had been so much as a mention of extra-marital sexual adventures involving the sovereign and his female subjects.

Charles's reigning mistress at the time of the Restoration, and for a good many years afterwards, was the former Barbara Villiers, whose husband, the Lord High Cuckold Roger Palmer, was created Earl of Castlemaine in 1661. Later in the reign she would be made Duchess of Cleveland in her own right. Barbara, nineteen years old when her royal lover returned to England, had already a number of sexual adventures to her credit and in the years to come was to accumulate a good many more; she was never faithful to the King for long at a time. Among her many lovers of later years were Charles Hart the actor, and Jacob Hall the tight-rope dancer. On one occasion, according to the gossip-writers, she was so attracted to the footman running beside her coach that she took him home and invited him to share her bath. As Andrew Marvell recorded with relish:

> Stripp'd to her skin, see how she stooping stands,
> Nor scorns to rub him down with those fair hands.

She was a lovely creature, with an exotic vitality that was as close to nymphomania as makes no matter. Yet in spite of her beauty, and the liberality with which she extended the hospitality of her bed to anybody who took her fancy, she was not a popular lady. Her amorous geniality was counterbalanced by a furious temper. She was jealous and grasping, and her manners were coarse.

Yet it was not all avarice, tantrums and sensuality. There was a certain spontaneous vivacity about her, and on occasions she could behave in an endearing manner. In the summer of 1662 King Charles brought his bride, Catherine of Braganza, to Whitehall by river. Pepys was among the crowd watching the procession of boats, and his diary contains a revealing passage:

> But that which pleased me best was that my Lady Castlemayne stood over against us upon a piece of White-hall—where I glutted myself with looking on her. But methought it was strange to see her Lord and her upon the same place, walking up and down without taking notice one of another; only, at first entry, he put off his hat and she made him a very civil salute—but afterwards took no notice one of another. But both of them now and then would take their child, which the nurse held in her armes, and dandle it. One thing more; there happened a scaffold to fall, and we feared some hurt but there was none; but she, of all the great ladies only, run down among the common rabble to see what hurt was done, and did take care of a child that received some little hurt; which methought was so noble.
>
> Anon there came one there, booted and spurred, that she talked long with. And by and by, she being in her haire, she put on his hat, which was but an ordinary one, to keep the wind off. But methought it became her mightily, as everything else do.

Needless to say, Charles's marriage to Catherine made no difference to his relations with Barbara.

Even in the early years Barbara was far from having a monopoly of the King's love-life, though she was the only one of his mistresses whose rank and position, in addition to the peculiar hold she had on his affections, gave her any strong influence on fashion or the affairs of the court. Two maids of honour, Jane Middleton and Winifred Wells, were among the first to enjoy his favours after the Restoration. Some years later he would cast his eye towards the theatre and take to his bed first Moll Davis and then Nell Gwyn, most famous of all his mistresses and the one who has most captivated the imagination of posterity. Later still would come the seductive

Breton Louise de Kéroualle, whom he created Duchess of Portsmouth and who alone rivalled Barbara Castlemaine for the extent of her influence.

For the moment, however, Barbara had it all her own way, and it was she, almost as much as the King, who set the moral tone of the court. Under the influence of the two of them the pursuit of love became the main preoccupation of the gallant lords and ladies who made up the society of Whitehall. From the rollicking pages of the Gramont memoirs it would appear that little else was ever thought of; and though allowance must be made for the personal inclinations of the born gossip-writer that was their author, Anthony Hamilton, there is no doubt that the double bed was the most important piece of furniture at the court of King Charles.

The second most popular indoor sport at Whitehall was gambling. Vast sums of money changed hands every night at the gaming-tables, and men and women would bet on anything. Cards were played for high stakes. The games were innumerable; Charles Cotton in his *Compleat Gamester* lists piquet, gleek, cribbage, whist, five-cards, plain-dealing, basset, and the Spanish game of ombre among many others. Anthony Hamilton mentions casually that Richard Talbot, who was later created Duke of Tyrconnel, lost three or four hundred guineas to the Comte de Gramont on the evening before he was put in the Tower. Even the lofty-minded Duke of Ormonde won and lost substantial sums.

The women of the court were equally addicted, and King Charles frequently had to fork out money to recoup Barbara Castlemaine's gambling losses. An exception to the general rule was Frances Stewart, the young court beauty to whom the King laid assiduous siege and who almost alone seems to have consistently resisted his advances. She was a simple, childlike creature whose tastes lay in more harmless directions. 'Blind-man's buff was the game she enjoyed most,' writes Hamilton; 'she built card castles while the deepest gambling was going on in her rooms, and there you saw the courtiers pressing round her, handing her cards or trying to imitate her skill in building.'

King Charles was not himself a great gambler, and indeed tried from time to time to discourage high stakes. But in his good-natured way he did not insist, and the gambling passions of his courtiers were not unduly interfered with. One of Charles's greatest interests, moreover, was horse-racing. He virtually created Newmarket as the fashionable centre it now became, and there betting reached its apogee.

The Royal Palace of Whitehall was not, of course, exclusively concerned with the court and its frivolities. The ramshackle group of buildings known collectively as the Palace also housed the seat of government. A few hundred yards away were the Houses of Parliament, but Parliament was not the effective centre of the country's administration. In the early years of the interregnum, before the establishment of the Cromwellian dictatorship, it had exercised real power, so far as a conglomeration of voluble individuals could ever be capable of doing so. But those days were over; the House of Commons had quickly subsided into being the subservient instrument of the Protectorate, and now, in 1660, the old regime had been restored, under which government was carried on by the King and his principal advisers, with reference to Parliament only when financial considerations made it necessary. Such at least was the intention, as it had been that of Charles I; as the reign of his son proceeded, the Commons, with control of the money-bags as their formidable weapon, would seek progressively to diminish the power of the King and increase their own.

In 1660, however, the Convention Parliament which had put its stamp of approval on the restoration of monarchy was concerned with little beyond the regularization of the royal constitution and was preparing for its own demise, to make way for a new body elected under the restored regime. The government of England was carried on by the Privy Council, or rather in practice by a smaller 'cabinet council' which was in fact a committee of the Council proper. And this body met regularly in Whitehall Palace under the chairmanship of the King. It comprised the principal officers of state. In earlier years the most influential of these had been the Lord Treasurer; William Cecil Lord Burghley, Queen Elizabeth's chief minister for forty years, had for most of that time held this office. Gradually, however, the Lord Chancellor had tended to over-shadow the Treasurer, and now this position was held by Sir Edward Hyde, who had been the King's chief adviser in the period leading up to the Restoration. He was nearer to being what in later centuries would be called Prime Minister than any statesman since Burghley. The Lord Treasurership still carried great prestige, but its holder at this time, Thomas Wriothesley Earl of Southampton, was without much drive or ambition. Other principal members of the inner council were the two Secretaries of State, Sir Edward Nicholas and General Monk's protégé Sir William Morrice. Monk himself, now Duke of Albemarle and Captain-General of the army, was another.

In the immediate aftermath of the Restoration King Charles was assiduous in his attendance at council meetings, even if it was the Chancellor who did most of the talking and had the leading part in making decisions. Some idea of how proceed-ings were conducted can be gleaned through the fortunate survival of a few informal notes that were passed across the table between King and Chancellor during the meetings.

'What do you think of my Lord Berkeley's being Deputy of Ireland, if we can find no better?' asked the King in one of these notes. 'Do you think we shall be rid of him by it?' was Hyde's rejoinder. 'For that is all the good of it.' King Charles stuck to his suggestion, but diplomatically: 'The truth of it is, the being rid of him doth incline me something to it; but when you have thought round, you will hardly find a fitter person.'

Another note from the King ran: 'I have been talking with the Scots lords about the business of that Kingdom and they find it most necessary that a secretary be named as I must do it to-morrow or next day.' Hyde's reply was revealing: 'I know not what to say to it, but I am sure you have so many things to think of that I wonder you can sleep.'

A more personal note crept in when, towards the end of 1660, the King's youngest and much-loved sister Minette paid a brief visit to England. She stayed at Tunbridge Wells, and Charles minuted to his Chancellor: 'I would willingly make a visit to my sister at Tunbridge for a night or two at farthest, when do you think I can best spare that time?' Hyde answered: 'I know no reason why you may not for such a time, (two nights) go the next week about Wednesday, or Thursday, and return time enough for the adjournment; which yet ought to be the week following. I suppose you will go with a light train?' To which King Charles replied: 'I intend to take nothing but my night bag.' This flippancy rather shocked the Chancellor, who scribbled back: 'Yes, you will not go without forty or fifty horse!' 'I count that part of my night bag,' replied the King.

These exchanges give a glimpse of how the government of England was carried on. The council administered the country. The King presided at its meetings, but at this stage of his reign, when he was feeling his way, he was usually ready to defer to the views of his chief minister. Lord Chancellor Hyde, a politician of long experience, great capacity and tireless industry, was the central figure of the administration and the real ruler of the kingdom.

In Parliament the peers, who had been in eclipse, sometimes partial and sometimes total, throughout the interregnum, now came into their own again. The balance between the two Houses was gradually shifting in favour of the Commons, and the process had been accelerated by the events of the preceding twenty years; but with the return of the old regime the House of Lords had a new lease of life. Many of the principal officers of state were themselves members of the Upper House, where they were able to give effect to royal policy; the ultimate power still resided in the great landed families.

Here the influence of the peerage extended beyond the confines of their own chamber. The burgesses who represented the cities and towns in the Commons were mostly merchants of wealth and substance; but the county members who made up the bulk of members were usually the younger sons of peers or in other ways subservient to the rural nobility. Powerful peers moreover were able to influence elections and ensure the return of their own nominees. The House of Commons in the reign of Charles II was essentially an aristocratic institution.

Whitehall, the Houses of Parliament and the Abbey were the central features of the city of Westminster. There was also St James's Park. This park had been known as such, an open space and recreation ground, for a century and more, but the form in which we see it today was essentially the creation of Charles II. To him it was a favourite haunt, and he gave it the stamp of his own personality. Before the year of the Restoration was out he set workmen to the task of making a canal through it, and though there have been changes since then this canal is in essence the St James's Park lake which to many generations has seemed one of the pleasantest spots in London. The King stocked the canal with water-fowl, the direct ancestors of the birds which in their beauty and variety give the lake its character and colour today. Charles II had a characteristically Stewart love of animals, and besides the birds the park under his auspices provided a home for deer, antelopes and sheep.

King Charles was devoted to his park, which ever since his time has been more closely associated with his memory than with that of any other of our sovereigns. Here the approachable monarch and his subjects met in an atmosphere of easy informality; the picture of Charles II that has remained most vivid in the mind of posterity is of the King sauntering through the park and along the Mall with his beloved spaniels at his heels, feeding the ducks and exchanging jokes with anybody who wished to talk to him. It is a picture that is in essence accurate. Charles was a great walker, and St James's Park was his favourite place of recreation.

It may be mentioned in passing that his plans for the canal or lake extended beyond the stocking of it with water-fowl. Among the gifts from abroad planned to celebrate the return of the monarchy was one that particularly appealed to his imagination; the Venetian Senate had had two ornate gondolas specially built for presentation to the King of England. Charles saw visions of a 'little Venice' in St James's Park, with gilded princes and lovely royal mistresses reclining on embroidered cushions in the splendid Italian vessels as they cruised up and down the canal. But he had over-estimated the possibilities, and the plan proved impracticable. The gondolas had a stormy passage when being taken by sea around the toe of Italy, and had to be sent back to Venice for repairs. They did at last arrive in the Thames in the summer of 1661, but it was found that the park lake was much too small to accommodate them. They eventually found a home at Hampton Court, where for some years they were used in state processions on the river.

Westminster represented the court, the government and the world of fashion. Separated from it along the Thames by the Strand, where stood the great houses of many of the nobility, was the City of London, an entity of its own, intensely independent, fiercely jealous of its rights, always capable of asserting its will against crown and parliament by means of the great wealth concentrated within its walls. It was this wealth that had played a decisive part in the outcome of the Great Civil War. In the earlier stages of the conflict the military advantage had lain persistently with the Royalists; but they failed to consolidate their successes in the field. In the war of attrition that ensued, economic realities gradually asserted their predominance. From first to last the City of London was on the side of the Parliament, and the funds supplied by the great merchants enabled a new army to be raised, trained, and above all paid, which proved too strong for royal forces weakened by Charles I's increasingly desperate shortage of money.

It was in this concentration of wealth that the power of

London lay: a power which no British government could afford to ignore. The city had been largely instrumental in overthrowing the old monarchy; it had now played an equally large part in restoring the King to his throne. In 1660 it was enthusiastically Royalist, but Charles II was never so strong as not to need the support of the London financiers, and in the later stages of his reign it was only his political skill and acumen that ensured that that support was forthcoming in sufficient strength to enable him to prevail against the machinations of those who were working to overthrow the Stewart regime.

The official entrance to the City of London in the west was at Temple Bar, the gateway that stood where Fleet Street met the Strand. And by ancient tradition the sovereign himself could not pass through this opening except by permission of the Lord Mayor and Corporation.

The walls of London still stood in some places, but they had long ceased to fulfil the function for which they were built —to mark the boundaries of the City and to make it a fortress which if necessary could stand a siege against a hostile army. Temple Bar itself was outside the walls, and London in the seventeenth century was constantly expanding in all directions. The size of its population is a matter of controversy, but most estimates put the figure for the City and suburbs somewhere in the region of 300,000 to 400,000; if Westminster is included the population may have been half a million, which would have been more than a tenth of that of England and Wales as a whole.

London within the walls, the City proper, was densely populated. It was a crowded town of narrow streets and medieval wooden buildings blotting out the sky with overhanging storeys. This congested area included a mass of small shops of every description, while cheek by jowl with the houses of the richer merchants, both in the City itself and in the suburbs, were countless hovels where the poorer citizens were huddled together in insanitary confusion.

The City was noisy as well as crowded. The cries of London, fascinating as they may seem in retrospect, made up an incessant babel; hawkers bawled the merits of their wares through the streets, while apprentices did the same for the benefit of the larger shops. The wheels of coaches and carts made a constant rattle on the cobbled roadways. London's traffic problems were quite as acute in the seventeenth as in the twentieth century. Hackney coaches abounded, and the problem was aggravated by the drivers' tendency to brawl and fight among themselves whenever a traffic block occurred, while they kept up a concurrent feud with the coachmen and footmen of the richer residents. All this was a constant headache for the urban authorities. In the autumn of 1660 a proclamation ordered 'that no Person of what estate, degree or quality soever, keeping or using any Hackney Coaches, or Coach-Horses, do from and after the 6th of November next, suffer the said Coaches and Horses or any of them to remain in the Streets or Passages of the Cities of London or Westminster to be there hired, but that they keep them within their respective Coach-houses, Stables or Yards.' But it had little effect.

Yet the London of the Restoration was not devoid of grandeur or dignity. Scattered among the low houses and shops were majestic buildings such as the Royal Exchange, where merchants from all over the world gathered daily to do business on a large scale, to hire shipping, and to discuss the news of the day: it was as much a place of social assembly as the centre of the nation's trade. More than a hundred parish churches, erected at different periods and some of them of great beauty, rose above the secular buildings, and supreme among them all was the splendid structure of St Paul's Cathedral, by far the largest church in England. Its greatest glories had passed. The spire had been burned down a century before, the nave was partly in ruins after years of neglect in the interregnum, and since the Reformation the church had been secularized to an astonishing degree; stalls were set up in the aisles, and its use as a meeting-place and gossip centre gave it more the air

Westminster: part of Wenceslaus Hollar's engraving of
the panorama of the City of London. Hollar, a consummate
draughtsman, was a Bohemian who had settled in England
by 1660.

Old London Bridge, by C. de Jongh. It had stood since the thirteenth century as the only London bridge across the Thames.

of a public hall than a place of worship. But it was still an impressive building, dominating the skyline of London.

St Paul's stood at the west end of the City proper. At the east end was an older if smaller edifice, the Tower of London, the formidable fortress built nearly 600 years before by William the Norman. The Tower had a long and macabre history as state prison and place of execution, and this part of its story was not yet done; but by 1660 its grimmest aspects lay in the past and it had become the show-place of London, famous above all for its menagerie where lions and other wild beasts were kept. Tourists visited the Tower with the eagerness that they show today, though not in such numbers; and guides regaled the gullible with such tales as have been not unknown in later ages. A Frenchman who toured the fortress in 1672 recorded having been shown 'William the Conqueror's musket, which is of such a length and thickness, that it is as much as a man can do to carry it on his shoulders.'

There was also London Bridge, as picturesque a structure as any to be seen in Britain. Since the thirteenth century it had stood as the only bridge across the Thames in the metropolitan area. Built on eighteen arches, it was lined with a double row of shops and houses, some of them of six storeys, far higher than their counterparts within the City. The turret at the southern end was customarily adorned with the heads of executed traitors, some of them dating back a century or more, left there until they rotted and fell.

The Thames was London's highway. The streets of the City might be narrow and insanitary, but the river was broad and comparatively clean. A constant succession of boats passed up and down, manned by the Thames watermen who constituted themselves the ruling body of the river and were renowned for their rough manners, their profanity of language and their gift of repartee.

The river was the scene of pageants that relieved the general drabness of life in the crowded city. Chief among them was the Lord Mayor's Show, which in those days usually took the

3

form of a procession of ornately decorated boats along the river. Lesser celebrations of the same order, both on the Thames and inland in the city, were held by the craft guilds. These festivities, dating back far into the Middle Ages, had previously had a religious basis; they were held on the feasts of the various saints to which each guild owed allegiance. But by the later seventeenth century they had been almost entirely secularized, while each vied with the others in the splendour of the ceremonies.

There were plenty of amusements available in Restoration London. With the end of Puritan rule the stage had come back into its own; two licensed theatres enjoyed the special patronage of the King and the Duke of York, while for the less sophisticated there were the unlicensed houses, the Red Bull and Sadlers' Wells, where the cruder type of melodrama catered for the multitude. Rougher entertainment still was provided in the gory garden arenas where bear-baiting, bull-baiting and cock-fighting took place. These unpleasant spec-tacles, contrary to wide belief, were not popular with all and sundry. Samuel Pepys, omnivorous in his appetite for new experiences and not noted for undue sensitivity, was disgusted though at the same time fascinated when he paid his first visit to the cockpit in Shoe Lane.

I soon had enough of it, [he wrote in his diary] and yet I would not but have seen it once, it being strange to observe the nature of those poor creatures, how they will fight till they drop down dead upon the table and strike after they are ready to give up the ghost—not offering to run away when they are wounded or weary past doing further. Where-as, where a Dunghill brood comes, he will, after a sharp stroke that pricks him, run off the stage, and then they wring off his neck without more ado. Whereas the other they preserve, though their eyes be both out, for breed only of a true cock of the game.

And when he bought his copy of *The Compleat Gamester*, in which Cotton somewhat surprisingly described cock-fighting as a sport 'full of delight and pleasure', Pepys added in the margin: 'and of Barbarity'.

Other ways in which the Londoner could amuse himself included watching the lunatics performing their antics in Bedlam and convicted harlots beating hemp or suffering under the lash in Bridewell. Taverns were innumerable, open all day and most of the night. Work started early for the average citizen, particularly in the summer; he would go to his office at dawn or thereabouts, toil for an hour or two, and then repair to the nearest tavern for his 'morning draught', which for men at least took the place of breakfast. He might well finish the day's work about noon; and after midday dinner he would have plenty of leisure for drinking during the remainder of the day.

Brothels were in plentiful supply. In Westminster there was one just behind the House of Lords, convenient for the nobility; in London Covent Garden and Drury Lane were noted centres for this oldest of trades. And across the river in Bankside there was a long row of houses of pleasure that had been famous for centuries.

Prostitution flourished gaily in the London of the Restoration, probably no more and no less than in most other periods. It had little relevance to the morals of the court, though the livelier wits of the day were at pains to show that both the ladies and their clients were indebted to the example set by their betters, and the royal mistresses were held up in pamphlets and broadsides as the patronesses of their more lowly sisters. A 'Humble address of the Ladies of Pleasure' to King Charles opened:

> We, your Majesty's most loyal and dutiful subjects, the Ladies of Pleasure in the several seraglios of Moorfields, Whetstone's Park, Lukener's Lane, Dog and Bitch Yard, and the rest of the stews and cony-burrows in and about the

virtuous Palace of Whitehall and the Cities of London and Westminster, being daily sensible of the great advantage we have reaped, under your Majesty's easy government, from the playhouses, masques, balls, serenades, Hyde Park and St James' night revels, publicly recommended and honoured by your Majesty's presence, and for the great licence and privilege we have enjoyed under your Majesty's Justices of the Peace, no ways inferior to those of the ladies of Rome or Venice, whereby those foolish things called wives are grown unfashionable and the keeping of a miss the principal character of a modish, well-bred gentleman: And having no less resentment of the honours some of our profession have received from your Majesty, in being promoted . . . to great titles . . . we do humbly beg leave to return our hearty thanks to your Majesty for all the said blessings . . . And we humbly assure ourselves of your Majesty's acceptance of this our zeal, which we will never be wanting to express as long as we are able to wag our tails, from the hands of our chiefs, the Duchess of Portsmouth and Madam Gwyn, whom we have prevailed with to present the same . . .

What Louise de Kéroualle, Duchess of Portsmouth, Charles II's French concubine, and her rival Nell Gwyn thought of such ribaldry is not recorded; from what we know of Nelly she might well have welcomed it, and would have been quite capable of replying in kind if she had been able to write. But when a similar libel, 'The poor-whores petition to the most splendid, illustrious, serene and eminent lady of pleasure, the Countess of Castlemayne', was printed in 1668, the great Barbara failed to see the joke. Pepys recorded that she was 'horribly vexed'.

Sexual pleasures were easy for the young London blades to find. They were also dangerous. Medical precautions were non-existent, and the more uninhibited literature of the time is full of the complaints of roisterers whose enjoyment had been rewarded with physical blight. A typical encounter is thus recorded:

> I lodged with her, I laid her down,
> I slept with her all night:
> I supped upon a cony fat
> Whose gravy was delight . . .
> She gave to me a syrup sweet
>   Was in her placket box,
> But ere three minutes went about
>   It proved the French pox . . .
> This fireship she did blow me up,
>   As my *effigies* shows,
> And all may read upon my face
>   The loss of teeth and nose.

Pepys has an anecdote of Lady Carnegie, the Duke of York's mistress—

> how her Lord, finding her and the Duke of York at the King's first coming in too kind, did get it out of her that he did dishonour him; and so he bid her continue to let him, and himself went to the foulest whore he could find, that he might get the pox; and did, and did give his wife it on purpose, that she (and he persuaded and threatened her that she should) might give it the Duke of York; which he did, and he did give it the Duchesse.

Pepys was an inveterate gossip, though this story went the rounds and was recorded by other authors. But there is no reliable evidence that either the Duke or his wife ever suffered from any venereal trouble.

The colour and pageantry of the great festivals brought life to the narrow streets; the brightness of innumerable shop signs concealed the drabness of the premises themselves, and the spires of the churches and the fine houses and courtyards

of the richer residents gave the city an air of dignity that was
the envy of other towns. And the green fields were close at
hand. The suburbs, or 'liberties', were extending the city's
tentacles, but to the north the open ground at Moorfields was
within easy walking distance; to the west Kensington and
Chelsea were still rustic villages; eastwards the countryside
led gracefully towards the coast; along the Strand between
London and Westminster the great houses and gardens of
the nobility made a majestic background to the Thames.

Yet when all is said and done the general atmosphere of
London was not pleasant. A heavy pall of smoke arose from
the furnaces used by the various tradesmen, and the cleaning
of the streets left much to be desired. The roadway was
frequently clogged with filth of every description. Horse-dung
was everywhere; nor were horses the only culprits. Public
sanitation was primitive, and the poorer classes were not
noticeably public-spirited in their personal habits. In short
the smell of the London streets hardly bears thinking about,
the babel was constant and deafening, and it is hardly surprising
that the more fastidious of mankind found the city a good
place to get out of. Too much should not be made of the poetry
of the time, for bards in all ages have extolled the virtues of
the country as against the town, but the tone is peculiarly
insistent in seventeenth-century England. Abraham Cowley,
a gentle and sensitive soul, reverted again and again to the
theme. In his poem *The Wish* he wrote:

> The very honey of all earthly joy
>   Does of all meats the soonest cloy,
>   And they (methinks) deserve my pity,
> Who for it can endure the stings,
> The Crowd, and Buzz, and Murmurings
>   Of this great Hive, the City.

And in *Of Solitude*:

Whilst this hard Truth I teach, methinks I see
  The Monster London laugh at me,
  I should at thee too, foolish City,
If it were fit to laugh at Misery,
  But thy Estate I pity.
Let but thy wicked men from out thee go,
  And all the Fools that crowd thee so,
  Even thou who dost thy Millions boast,
A Village less than Islington wilt grow,
  A Solitude almost.

At a somewhat earlier date Thomas Randolph, a more robust character, had written:

Come spurre away,
  I have no patience for a longer stay;
    But must go downe,
And leave the chargeable noise of this great Towne.
  I will the country see,
    Where old simplicity,
      Though hid in gray
      Doth looke more gay
Than foppery in plush and scarlet clad.
    Farewell you City-wits that are
      Almost at Civil war;
Tis time that I grow wise, when all the
    world grows mad.

Sir Richard Fanshawe, a courtier and a diplomat, wrote more specifically:

  Who would pursue
The smoky glory of the Town,
That may go till his native Earth,
And by the shining Fire sit down
  Of his own hearth,

Free from the griping Scriveners Bands,
And the more biting Mercers Books;
Free from the bait of oyled hands
    And painted looks?

Yet by no means all poets felt this way. Dryden, the leading figure of Restoration literature, was as urban in his tastes as urbane in his outlook, the monarch of the theatre and the sage of Will's coffee house; and the rising court wits, Sedley and Etherege and Rochester, were townsmen first and last.

No other town in England approached the capital in size or social importance. Norwich and Bristol came next, but the population of neither amounted to a tenth of that of London. These and other leading urban centres, however, played a vital part in the affairs of the nation, and it would be quite wrong to dismiss any English provincial town as a London in miniature. Each had a character of its own; indeed there was far more individuality among them than at the present day, when rapid communication and continual shifts in population have produced a uniformity unknown to our forefathers. Roads in the later seventeenth century were in many cases not much better than they had been in the Middle Ages, and the prevalence of highway robbers made journeys things to avoid if possible. The generality of the population, as opposed to the gentry, never moved beyond the confines of their own locality. In these circumstances each town remained an isolated community, with its own character developed over the centuries, its own jurisdiction and its own customs, having little contact with the distant world of London and Westminster. Each also had almost its own language. The educated classes spoke the local dialect rather than the cultivated speech of Westminster or Oxford, and a burgher of Exeter would hardly have been able to make himself understood by his counterpart in Newcastle. The lords lieutenant of counties and the local sheriffs exercised administration with little interference from the central government.

With such diversity of character it is impossible to generalize, and equally impossible to go into detail concerning social life in the various communities. Under the general heading of English towns there were various types into which they can be broadly divided. There were the great trade centres such as Bristol, Norwich and Newcastle. York was in a position of its own, having from time immemorial been not only the seat of England's second archbishopric but virtually the capital of the north. There were the old county capitals such as Taunton and Devizes, cathedral cities with old traditions such as Canterbury, Ely and Salisbury. And there were the small market towns scattered over the country, insignificant in population but ranking as more than villages; each with a local pride and intense individuality.

Second to London in population, among the cities and towns of England, was Norwich, for centuries the centre of the wool trade which in the Middle Ages had provided a substantial portion of the wealth of the country. In the sixteenth century Norwich had suffered something of a decline, but in the seventeenth, through the development of the textile trade coupled with local enterprise in new industries, it took on a new lease of life and was now a thriving community. As the undisputed capital of East Anglia it possessed a pride and character of its own; yet in some ways it resembled London more closely than many of its kind. Sometimes described as 'a lesser London', it boasted a mayoral inauguration ceremony rivalling the Lord Mayor's Show of the metropolis, and its guild celebrations were on a similar scale. A cathedral city of charm and beauty, it had a social life which could bear comparison with that of Westminster.

East Anglia had throughout the Civil War been a Roundhead stronghold; this meant at least that Norwich had been on the winning side. Like the City of London it had by its wealth contributed to the Commonwealth victory; it had been allowed to develop its fortunes undisturbed by any fighting on its doorstep. Nor did the Restoration place it under a cloud. A rich and aristocratic community had no need to apologize for its Republican background. Cultured and self-assured, it throve both socially and intellectually. Its most illustrious citizen was the famous physician and author Sir Thomas Browne.

Third in population came Bristol, trade centre of the west and more influential than Norwich in the affairs of the country. Like London Bristol was a major seaport, and its position in the world of overseas trade gave Bristol society a peculiarly cosmopolitan flavour. The early Spanish and Portuguese explorers involved in the discovery of America, including Christopher Columbus himself, had had connections with the port; John Cabot actually sailed from Bristol on his voyages to the New World. The city's company of Merchant Venturers had developed a diverse and flourishing commerce with southern Europe, and traders from almost every country in the known world were familiar figures in Bristol's streets and taverns.

The great western city had played a key part in the Civil War, changing hands twice after important military actions. When Prince Rupert took it by storm in 1643 it became a vital factor in Royalist strategy, Charles I's one great outlet to the world beyond. When the same commander surrendered it to Sir Thomas Fairfax, finding the city indefensible, it was the final nail in King Charles's political coffin, and it brought about the disgrace of Rupert, his most distinguished general.

War and devastation had enhanced rather than damaged the reputation of Bristol. Its importance as a western centre and seaport had been amply demonstrated, and it stood in the public eye as the second city in the kingdom. Its atmosphere was one of bustling, international, highly commercial activity, and its society reflected its interests. As much as any town in England it took an independent line in managing its own affairs.

Exeter, deep in the south-west, and Newcastle-upon-Tyne, in the extreme north, were others that could be placed under the general heading of provincial capitals. Exeter, an old

Roman city, was like Norwich a centre of the cloth trade. Newcastle, once a station on the Roman Wall, depended mainly on coal. Each had been of military importance in past ages: Exeter a bastion against the unruly Cornish, almost a foreign race; Newcastle for centuries a fortress against the Scots. The population of Exeter at this time has been estimated at some 12,000; Newcastle's was roughly the same, or perhaps a little more. These figures compared with the 20,000 to 30,000 of Bristol and Norwich.

Newcastle was exceptional among England's largest towns in not being the seat of a bishopric. Cathedral cities, owing their prominence to their status as centres of ecclesiastical life rather than of commerce, were scattered through the country. The cathedrals of England, built mostly in the thirteenth and fourteenth centuries, were the glory of the land. From each radiated a tradition of gracious existence under the authority of its bishop. Lincoln and Salisbury, Ely and Wells, Durham and Lichfield, testified to the continuing influence of the Christian ethos on English life.

By far the most important of these cities was York. Its history alone was enough to set it apart. In Roman times the city of Eboracum was the centre of social life and government in the north of England. The Emperor Constantius Chlorus had died in the city in 306, and his son Constantine the Great was proclaimed there as his successor. As a centre of Christianity York was almost as old. Its bishop was the senior of the three British prelates present at the Council of Arles in 314, and when the new Christian mission was sent to England by Pope Gregory the Great at the end of the sixth century, the Archbishopric of York was founded within a few years of that of Canterbury.

This peculiar position as England's second capital, in both a political and an ecclesiastical sense, the city of York had never lost. In all the major crises of the country's history it had been a key centre, from the Danish and Norman invasions (its capture by Harold Hardrada in 1066 was the vital prelude to the Battle of Hastings) to the Great Civil War, when it withstood a long siege under the Marquess of Newcastle before falling into Roundhead hands after the Royalist defeat at Marston Moor. Throughout the Middle Ages it had been continuously the seat of government in the north, and the future King Richard III made his reputation as soldier and statesman there when, as Duke of Gloucester, he made it his seat of administration. In Henry VIII's reign the city's political status was put on a regular footing by the creation of the Council of the North under a Lord President, an office which was held in the sixteenth and seventeenth centuries by some of the greatest men in England, the last and most famous being Thomas Wentworth Earl of Strafford.

Smaller in population than Norwich and Bristol, York was thus of more truly national importance than either of them. It was indeed a commercial centre, largely connected like Norwich with the cloth trade; but industry was not its main concern. City life revolved around the Minster, one of Britain's most splendid architectural monuments: an edifice of more importance in its setting than Westminster Abbey or St Paul's Cathedral, because more isolated in its grandeur. The Archbishop and the officials of the Minster were leaders of York society, a society which embodied the atmosphere of a capital city which York at all times possessed. At the moment of the Restoration both city and Minster were recovering from the wounds inflicted by civil war and its aftermath; but recovery was rapid. Serene and secure in its independence, York quickly recovered its eminence as the kingdom's second capital.

Canterbury, seat of the Primate of All England, was in comparison with York a minor city. Dominated by the Cathedral, as impressive a structure as York Minster, its importance was ecclesiastical and cultural. It was a city of great beauty and venerable tradition, but it was too near to London and Westminster to play the part of a provincial capital; nor was it anything like the size of its northern counterpart.

Both England's archiepiscopal cities were centres of education, as indeed were most towns which could boast an old cathedral. Schools in the Middle Ages had grown up in the shadow of religious communities. Education was the prerogative of the Church, and it was not recognized that literacy was necessary for the layman. Thus the early schools were largely in the nature of seminaries, established to provide recruitment for the clergy. This is not to say that, even in the earliest times, there was no lay element; but in the higher ranks of society such education as was thought necessary was supplied privately by resident chaplains in the great houses.

The Reformation brought a change. With the suppression of the monasteries those schools that depended on them either disappeared or were refounded as lay institutions by the monarch or a local magnate, while new foundations made their appearance. Henry VIII, Edward VI and Elizabeth I all played their part in founding and refounding schools, which in the process changed their character. They no longer existed for the benefit of 'poor scholars' destined for a clerical career; the 'public schools' became the preserve of the wealthier classes, and the nobility took to sending their sons to school in preparation for higher education at the universities or the inns of court.

Many of the old ecclesiastical schools continued their existence under the new order, and among them were those of the two senior cathedral cities. King's School, Canterbury, and St Peter's, York, still contend for the title of England's oldest school. It is impossible to resolve the question, but there is no need to dispute the fact that the honour belongs to one or the other of them. In all probability there were schools attached to the Cathedral and the Minster almost from their foundation; nor is their continuity in much doubt.

These two schools, however, were not, socially speaking, among the foremost in the seventeenth century. The public schools which had now become fashionable were scattered among towns large and small throughout the country. Shrewsbury, Rugby and Tonbridge were among those that were coming to the fore. Winchester, once the capital of Wessex and England but now a typical cathedral city, could boast probably the oldest college with a continuous recorded history.

There were, however, two schools which, so far as social considerations went, stood out above the rest. These were Eton and Westminster. Eton, founded by Henry VI, stood close to Windsor Castle and owed its supremacy to its royal neighbourhood and the patronage of the sovereign. Westminster also had the advantage of proximity to the court, but at the time of the Restoration its reputation had been gained even more by the enormous prestige attaching to the name of its redoubtable headmaster, Richard Busby. Dr Busby was one of the most formidable figures of seventeenth-century England. His reign at Westminster lasted for fifty-seven years; he had taken office in turbulent circumstances in 1638, being confirmed in his post two years later, and he continued as headmaster till his death at the age of eighty-nine in 1695. During that time he built up a reputation enjoyed by no other pedagogue before or since. His was an overpowering personality, and stories about him are innumerable. When Charles II visited the school he asked (and was given) the King's permission to keep his hat on in the royal presence, lest his pupils should think that there was any person more important than himself. He flogged all and sundry with cheerful and unfailing vigour. A tale is recorded of how a French visitor was innocently watching some young Westminsters playing football in Little Dean's Yard when the ball went through the window of the headmaster's room. Busby emerged in a fury to demand the identity of the culprit, and the boys to save their skins pointed to the Frenchman. Without further inquiry Busby hauled the protesting tourist into his study and gave him six of the best.

However arbitrary his methods, Busby was a great scholar and a magnificent teacher. Those who wanted the best education for their children were eager to entrust them to his care, even though they might themselves have vivid memories of sufferings under his lash. His success was shown in the eminence achieved by his pupils in later life. John Dryden, Christopher Wren, Charles Sackville Earl of Dorset, John Locke and Matthew Prior were all at Westminster under Busby.

The university towns, Oxford and Cambridge, stood somewhat apart from the general run of urban communities. Life therein was dominated, to a greater degree than now, by the academic institutions in their midst. In size they were roughly equivalent, each having a population of rather less than 10,000; and this figure included some 3,000 undergraduates at Oxford and 2,500 at Cambridge. With so large a proportion of the inhabitants being directly connected with the university, the élite of the locality, it was obvious that the civil corporation would play second fiddle; and it was in fact the university authorities who governed Oxford and Cambridge. As regards the undergraduates, town-and-gown rivalry existed then as always, not infrequently exploding in riot; but it was usually gown that came uppermost.

Undergraduates do not differ greatly through the centuries. Then as now there were those who devoted themselves earnestly to their studies, with a view to furthering their future careers, either professional or academic; and there were others, usually those more blessed with worldly goods, who saw in their three or four years at the university a glorious opportunity for drinking, gambling and whoring. As with the public schools, the original ecclesiastical atmosphere of the universities had largely evaporated. The 'poor scholars' destined for the church had given place to youths from upper class and upper middle-class families whose fathers sent them to Oxford and Cambridge to prepare them for life and society and to give them the polish and culture that a university might be expected to provide. At the same time the poorer classes were not excluded, though their status was somewhat invidiously emphasized. Three grades of undergraduates were more or less officially recognized: those of upper commoner (the nobility), gentleman commoner, and servitor. The servitors, boys whose parents could not afford to pay for their education, compounded the fees by waiting on the dons and on the wealthier undergraduates.

The average age for entering the university was fifteen. Undergraduates were thus equivalent in maturity to modern schoolboys, though in an age of precocity they were a good deal more emancipated. Their parents naturally expected them to be rigidly controlled, in matters of discipline and instruction, by the dons who had them in care. In practice the amount of control exercised varied very much according to the individual character of the don concerned. Some fellows of colleges took this duty very seriously; others could not be bothered with undergraduates but devoted all their time to their own studies or, in not a few cases, to raffish amusements more generally associated with their pupils.

On the whole the cause of education and scholarship may be said to have flourished at the universities. Boys came up from school with a good grounding in the classics, and the university curriculum was first and foremost classical. At the same time theology was widely taught at Oxford, and mathematics at Cambridge. Philosophy, metaphysics and the natural sciences found their place. The dons included many scholars of the first order, and Oxford and Cambridge were truly the intellectual capitals of the country.

Both towns had been of great importance in the Great Civil War, but Oxford more so. For most of the period it had been the political and military capital of Royalist England. Charles I had lived and held court at Christ Church, while Queen Henrietta Maria had resided at Merton. Naturally research and study had been sadly disrupted, but at the same time Oxford had acquired increased political and fashionable stature. The role of Cambridge had been more modest, but as a centre of Puritan and Roundhead activity it had benefited from being on the winning side. Oliver Cromwell, the main victor of the war, was a Cambridge man, who always looked with a benevolent eye on his old university.

In the capital the universities had to some extent their

counterpart in the inns of court. Gray's Inn, Lincoln's Inn and the Temple, headquarters of the legal profession, catered, so far as training facilities were concerned, for the sons of country gentry as well as lawyers. It was essential for a future land-owner to have some education in the law, and the inns in the seventeenth century were widely regarded as a third university. The law student and the undergraduate differed little in status or general outlook. As in the universities, there were numbers of rich young men in the inns who had little intention of doing any serious work and who looked on their period of training as an opportunity to sample the fleshpots. In both institutions there was plenty of rowdiness; yet here both undergraduates and law students were eclipsed by the apprentices. These youths, pupils attached to particular trades and the craft guilds, abounded in all large towns and were prominent in all events that provided an excuse for rioting. Like their successors, the so-called 'students' of the present day, they assumed the privilege of making nuisances of themselves in aid of causes that did not concern them. The apprentices of London were particularly notorious.

The towns however, thriving and populous as many of them were, full of life and character, were not the essence of England. The nation was primarily agricultural, and its heart was in the countryside. Merchants in the towns might keep the wheels of industry turning, but it was the farm labourers in the country who produced the basic materials that made up England's wealth. Roads were bad and transport primitive, and each village was an isolated community, cut off from its neighbours and knowing and caring little of what went on in the community beyond its boundaries. In a period when the average villager never moved more than a few miles from his home, the greatest figure in his scheme of things was the village constable. The sheriffs and the justices of the peace in the county town were remote figures whose authority seldom impinged on his existence.

In the tiny, mainly self-contained community that was the

English village, the ancient ecclesiastical organization still held sway. The administrative unit was the parish; it was the parish officials who regulated the details of daily life. Local government was democratic; every householder was liable to be called upon to serve in the capacity of one or other of the parish officers. The village constable, responsible for law and order, was one of these; others were the churchwardens, the overseers of the poor and the overseers of the highways. Between them these officials, unpaid and responsible to the Lord Lieutenant and the justices in the county town, carried on the government of the community, dealt with disputes over land and social life, suppressed malefactors, and watched over the welfare of the individual. The incumbent of the parish held a somewhat nebulous position in the secular sphere, but socially he was the most influential figure in village existence.

The villager's life was one of considerable hardship. At all times it was one of constant toil to make ends meet, and he was much at the mercy of the weather. A bad harvest could mean conditions bordering on starvation, and among the labouring classes unemployment was widespread. Here the parish officers bore a heavy responsibility, for poor relief was on a local basis. These officers inclined towards harshness in their dealings with the poor; not unnaturally, since there were a great many poor and funds were severely limited. Heavy penalties were available. The able-bodied who could but did not work met with little compassion, and the vagrant was liable to whipping. And if the parish could drive an undesirable out to be somebody else's responsibility, it leaped at the opportunity. Thus some unfortunates found themselves driven from parish to parish in increasing destitution and with no diversion other than periodical floggings.

The more well-to-do households were mostly self-sufficient. They made their own clothes, grew their own food and brewed their own beer. The family was a closely-knit unit. Marriages were arranged by parents, though less rigidly than among the richer classes; such marriages might turn out badly, but even when they did husband and wife usually stuck together for economic reasons. Divorce was unknown (except in the highest circles where it might occasionally be arranged by act of Parliament), and the united labour of father, mother and children was necessary to keep the home going. In an average household the number of children was probably four to five. Many more than these came into the world; birth control had not been thought of, but infant mortality was high.

Plague was an ever-current menace. Three centuries earlier the whole country had been devastated by one of the most terrible outbreaks recorded in history. Since the Black Death there had been no such general visitation, and the pestilences that from time to time swept through the overcrowded towns had less effect on the open countryside. But primitive sanitation, coupled with lack of such medical knowledge as existed in larger communities, meant a heavy mortality when the plague did strike.

Yet in spite of toil, pestilence and famine, the Restoration countryman contrived to enjoy himself. His was an unsophisticated existence, and the immemorial pleasures of the countryside were enough to keep him amused. Music and dancing had their place in all but the humblest homes. Field-sports were not the sole prerogative of the rich; shooting and hare-hunting were within the reach of all. There were plenty of games to play; probably the most popular was football, which, though frowned upon by authority, gave an outlet for the animal spirits of a rough and virile population. Whole villages would play; there were virtually no rules, and injuries were manifold; to say nothing of riots into which a fierce game almost inevitably developed.

Cricket, a less violent game than football, was played mainly in the south of England. Its origins are obscure, and its history before 1700 a subject of considerable controversy; but enough evidence exists to show that it was popular in Sussex, Kent and Surrey in the days of the Stewarts. It has been suggested that the development of the game owed much to Royalist courtiers on the run who hid in the country during the interregnum and became acquainted for the first time with the curious ritual of bat and ball which had been familiar for centuries to rustic communities. Fascinated by this most distinctively English of games, the gentry (according to this theory) introduced it after the Restoration to more sophisticated circles; thence developed the era of the great patrons who in the eighteenth century made cricket an essential part of English life and transformed it into the great national game as played today.

Tennis, the other aristocrat among games, was associated more with the towns and with the upper classes, and was more cosmopolitan in its history and popularity. Its origins are believed to have been in France, and the curious design of its court to have developed from the cloisters of medieval monasteries. By the seventeenth century it was popular over most of Europe, and had assumed the form in which it still exists as a somewhat esoteric sport, dwarfed by its offspring lawn tennis. Few games have changed so little over the centuries. Tennis was a truly royal pastime. Most English kings from Henry VIII onwards played it, and Charles II himself was a keen and expert performer.

Hunting and horse-racing were likewise mainly the preserve of the upper classes. Fox-hunting had not yet attained its predominance among field-sports, but deer were hunted by the major landowners in most parts of the country. In racing King Charles II's patronage is a matter of history. At his beloved Newmarket, which under him became the headquarters of the sport, he built himself a house, imported Arab stallions, and put the whole business on a national footing. The town became one of the King's favourite resorts, and he made for it whenever he could get away from the cares of kingship.

Hunting and racing, together with shooting, made up a large part of the occupations of England's country gentry, whose lives in general did not differ much, apart from the matter of affluence, from those of countrymen on a lower level. The squire might be an awe-inspiring figure to the yeoman or villager; sometimes perhaps something of a tyrant. But he spoke the same dialect, enjoyed the same pleasures, followed the same agricultural pursuits if on a larger scale, and was equally oblivious of the world of culture. True, a certain number of squires played a part in the nation's counsels, either in the Lords or Commons, and were thus a link between the government at Westminster and the common people of the counties; but the majority of country gentry, while serving as justices of the peace and playing their part in local government, seldom looked far beyond the confines of their own demesnes. Books played little part in their scheme of things. Many, without doubt, were as illiterate as the labourers on their estates.

There were colourful ceremonies in England's rural communities, going back through the Christian centuries to immemorial folk traditions. Christmas, May Day and harvest-time saw the rustics in their best attire, revelling in the simple joys that had delighted their ancestors through the ages. Herrick, writing rather earlier in the century, paints a charming picture of a village celebration of Harvest Home:

See, here a *Maukin*, there a sheet,
As spotlesse pure, as it is sweet;
The Horses, Mares, and frisking Fillies,
(Clad all in Linnen, white as Lillies),
The Harvest Swaines, and Wenches bound
For joy, to see the *Hock-cart* crown'd.
About the Cart, heare, how the Rout
Of Rural Younglings raise the shout;
Pressing before, some coming after,
Those with a shout, and these with laughter.
Some blesse the Cart; some kisse the sheaves;
Some prank them up with Oaken leaves;
Some crosse the Fill-horse; some with great
Devotion, stroak the home-borne wheat:

While other Rusticks, lesse attent
To Prayers, then to Merryment,
Run after with their breeches rent.
Well, on, brave boyes, to your Lords Hearth,
Glitt'ring with fire; where, for your mirth,
Ye shall see first the large and cheefe
Foundation of your Feast, Fat Beefe:
With Upper Stories, Mutton, Veale
And Bacon, (which makes full the meale)
And sev'rall dishes standing by,
As here a Custard, there a Pie,
And here all tempting Frumentie.
And for to make the merry cheere,
If smirking Wine be wanting here,
There's that, which drowns all care, stout Beere. . .

Herrick's lines give an unforgettable impression of good cheer
and good viands, which may well have been far from the general
line of existence. But the country folk in normal times did do
themselves well in such creature comforts as were available to
them. Apart from times of famine, fresh food was abundant and
cheap. There was normally a good supply of meat, and beer
was plentiful at prices which all could afford. And in the West
Country there was cider.

Weddings were among the most popular day-to-day celebrations. They were constantly taking place, and in the cases
of rich and poor the procedure was much the same, differing
only in degree. The seventeenth-century wedding was a rumbustious affair abounding in sturdy ribaldry, which culminated
in the bride being ceremoniously undressed and the couple
seen to bed by all the guests. Everybody was gaily dressed,
with coloured scarves and ribbons, and everybody got drunk.
'We saw Sir Richard and his fine Lady wedded,' wrote a
correspondent when Sir Richard Temple was married, 'and
flung the stocking, and then left them to themselves, and so in
this manner was ended the celebration of his Marriage à la

mode; after that we had Musick, Feasting, Drinking, Revelling, Dancing, and Kissing: it was Two of the Clock this morning before we gott Home.'

Marriage among the poor took place comparatively late. A young man had to be established in life and able to give his bride a home before he could wed, and this might be when he was well on in his twenties. But the oldest sport of all flourished as abundantly as in most ages. The English village was far removed from the lascivious atmosphere of the Restoration court, but then as now the highest and the lowest took a similarly tolerant attitude towards sexual morality; no great blame was attached to a village girl who might stray from the path of chastity. A wedding in church might have to wait, but many a joyful union was consummated in wood or field. The authorities indeed came down heavily on the consequences that were liable to ensue. Here was another headache for the parish, for its officers might have to pay for the upbringing of a bastard. An erring maid might even find herself in the stocks. But both the parish records and the many semi-pornographic verses that circulated in Restoration England indicate that human nature was continually triumphing over official disapproval. No local Bumble could deprive rural England of its favourite amusement.

Such, in broad outline, was the state of rural English life at the time of King Charles's return. It was not noticeably different from conditions prevailing when his grandfather had left Scotland for his new inheritance. Puritan oppression had not succeeded in rooting out the old traditions and pleasures of the countryside.

Literature and the Stage

Tell me, O tell, what kind of thing is Wit,
Thou who Master art of it . . .
A thousand different shapes it bears,
Comely in thousand shapes appears.
Yonder we saw it plain; and here 'tis now,
Like Spirits in a Place, we know not How.

Abraham Cowley

English literature in the time of the later Stewarts had a character all its own—sharply distinguished from that of the eras that preceded and followed it. In popular estimation its essence lies in 'Restoration comedy', which with its wit and cynicism is held to epitomize the age of Charles II; and, though this is too narrow a reading of what was in fact a literature of opulence and variety, the emphasis is not unjust. For in the seventeenth century dramatic writing had a prominence which it has never since been able to boast.

For this the Elizabethan age was responsible. The secular theatre was a new phenomenon in the sixteenth century, however much it may have owed to the mystery plays performed at religious festivals in the Middle Ages, and when there came the splendid blossoming of English literature led by Marlowe and Shakespeare, its exponents made the fullest use of the new medium. The age saw the rudimentary formation of the English novel as well as the philosophical writings of Bacon; but it was the drama and dramatic poetry that above all gave Elizabethan literature its lustre and its vitality.

This flowering of literary activity actually reached its culmination after the great Queen's death. Marlowe was a pure Elizabethan, but Shakespeare, though he is usually regarded as such, in fact produced nearly all his greatest work in the reign of James I. Beaumont and Fletcher were likewise Jacobeans, and Shakespeare's natural successor, Ben Jonson, who to most contemporaries shone as the more illustrious writer of the two, was virtually Poet Laureate to King James (the post did not officially exist till later in the century.) With the active encouragement of England's most intellectual monarch, literature flourished as never before; and it continued to find its principal outlet in the theatre.

This aspect of literary culture met with a temporary stoppage in the Civil War and the interregnum. The Puritans frowned on the theatre and persecuted stage-players, and the times were hardly propitious for imaginative work such as had flourished in the previous age. A fair quantity of good poetry flowed from the pens of Cavalier bards, and a lesser supply from those of their opponents, but such literature as was produced consisted mainly of pamphlets and sermons. Prose, not poetry, was the literary keynote of the age.

With the Restoration the stage came back into its own. The King and his brother James were enthusiastic patrons of the theatre, and two new houses were quickly opened for the King's and the Duke of York's companies of actors, under Thomas Killigrew and Sir William Davenant. The influence on the literature of the age of this royal patronage, together with the development of a more sophisticated stage and the advent of actresses, will be discussed in greater detail later. Here it may be said that, after an interval in which writing had taken a different course, the old order was restored and the theatre became once again the central vehicle for authorship.

The playwrights of the early years of the seventeenth century produced work that has maintained its pre-eminence to the present day. They were poets first, dramatists second. Strength and sublimity in verse were their aims in tragedy; the humour of their comedies, where prose alternated with verse, was of a rowdy, rumbustious nature, which a later age might characterize as slapstick. In all their work there was a gusto that was part of the spirit of Elizabethan times. They wrote with glorious carelessness, and they altered each other's texts with a ruthless freedom which often makes it difficult for scholars to make out who wrote what.

All this was alien to the thought of the Restoration age. The emphasis now was on *wit*. The word had a wider application than one associates with it today; it meant far more than the expression of ideas in a neat and epigrammatic form such as is generally understood by the word *wit* today. It is not possible to define with any degree of accuracy. Cowley made an attempt in a characteristically whimsical poem, and could achieve only the despairing interrogation:

> What is it then, which like the Power Divine
> We only can by Negatives define?

Wit certainly did not signify frivolity. Restoration tragedy has left less of a mark than Restoration comedy, but tragedy still ruled as the senior branch of dramatic writing, and most of the acknowledged wits who wrote comedies turned out plays in a loftier style as well. What wit did as a rule imply was facility of expression, intellectual ability, and elegance of mind. To quote Cowley again:

> In a true piece of Wit all things must be,
> Yet all things there agree.

It was in this emphasis on wit, the insistence on elegance in writing, on tidiness of mind, that the age differed from its predecessor. Jacobean extravagance of language, the careless-ness regarding time and place of Shakespeare and his contem-poraries, found little echo in the plays of Charles II's reign. There was both loss and gain in the change. Dryden, the pre-eminent wit of his time, towards the end of his writing life expressed the difference admirably:

> Strong were our Syres, and as they fought they Writ,
> Conqu'ring with Force of Arms and Dint of Wit:

Theirs was the Giant Race before the Flood;
And thus, when Charles Return'd, our Empire stood.
Like Janus, he the stubborn Soil manur'd,
With Rules of Husbandry the Rankness cur'd;
Tam'd us to Manners when the Stage was rude,
And boisterous English Wit with Art indu'd . . .
Our Age was cultivated thus at length,
But what we gain'd in Skill we lost in Strength.

It is noteworthy that Dryden in this passage, even while deprecating the rudeness and lack of skill of the earlier dramatists, still uses the all-embracing term 'wit' in describing their achievement; which makes it harder than ever to confine the word within any narrow meaning.

At an earlier period Dryden, writing of himself in the prologue to one of his plays, *Aureng-Zebe*, expresses much the same sentiment:

What Verse can do he has perform'd in this,
Which he presumes the most correct of his;
But spite of all his pride, a secret shame
Invades his Breast at Shakespeare's sacred name:
Aw'd when he hears his Godlike Romans rage,
He in a just despair would quit the Stage;
And to an Age less polish'd, more unskill'd,
Does with disdain the foremost Honours yield.

Needless to say, there was no abrupt change in 1660 from one type of writing to another. Certainly Charles II and his followers brought with them French fashions in literature as in other aspects of life; Racine and Molière became models for English writers rather than Shakespeare and Jonson. But all ages are ages of transition, and as the heroics of the early seventeenth century had merged into the solemnities of the Puritan era, so did these imperceptibly develop into the cheerful elegances of the Restoration period, which themselves prepared the way for what is known as the Augustan Age of the early eighteenth century.

At the time of the King's return, moreover, some of the most eminent figures of earlier days were still writing. Towering over them all was John Milton. For so illustrious an author, Milton was a strangely unattractive character. A fanatical and humourless Puritan, he had in the dozen or so years before 1660 restricted his writing mainly to the production of polemical tracts in support of the Republican cause and in denunciation of its enemies, varied with treatises in favour of divorce after his own first marriage had broken down; characteristically Milton, an uncompromising egoist, advocated the freedom of a husband to divorce an incompatible wife, never that of a wife to get rid of her husband. None of these works was negligible from the literary point of view; Milton was incapable of writing undistinguished English, either in prose or verse. But the products of his political period make depressing reading.

Yet in his earlier years, his 'Cavalier' period, this narrow, proselytizing bigot had poured forth poetry of a sublimity unequalled except by Shakespeare, much of it characterized by a charm and a lightness of touch worthy of Beaumont or Herrick. In *L'Allegro* and *Il Penseroso* he portrayed nature and the countryside in cadences of unforgettable loveliness, while *Lycidas*, in its form a conventional lament for a dead friend, is arguably the finest single poem in the English language, marred though it is by the insertion of an irrelevant diatribe against 'our corrupted Clergy' (one of his pet hates) more characteristic of his later writings. A dedicated classical scholar with an unrivalled sense of words and a marvellous gift for imagery, Milton brought his native tongue as near to perfection as can be achieved.

All this was laid aside at the advent of the grim times that marked the middle period of the poet's life, during which he wrote little verse except for a few sonnets. But germinating in his mind were the ideas for his most impressive work of all, the series of epics on the grand scale which would come to fruition in an age to which his spirit was wholly antipathetic.

It might have been thought that at the Restoration Milton would have been one of the first victims of Royalist revenge. He had been one of the most virulent pamphleteers of the Cromwellian era; as 'Secretary for Foreign Tongues' he had been a member, albeit a minor one, of the Republican government; he had vigorously defended the beheading of Charles I; he had attacked monarchy and the Royalist cause with all the vigour of his brilliant pen, and he had continued to do so till the very eve of the revival of the old regime. He was never lacking in courage, and he almost certainly expected the worst.

In the event he was let off extremely lightly. His case was discussed, and he did not lack enemies who wished him dead. But though his name was not excepted from the list of those to be pardoned, and though he was actually arrested, his imprisonment was brief. Thereafter he was left to continue his writing unmolested.

There is no evidence that this was in recognition of his position as England's greatest poet, though if King Charles was personally responsible for the line taken this may well have weighed with him. But very probably he was simply considered to be politically unimportant, not dangerous to the monarchy. In any case the tolerance with which he was treated did credit to the restored administration.

Milton was totally blind by the time of the Restoration, and he had his domestic troubles, mainly concerned with his unsatisfactory relationship with his daughters. But on the whole his last years were tranquil, and in the course of them he produced his greatest work. In one way at least the Restoration, of which he so strongly disapproved, was a godsend to him. Courageously recalcitrant though he was, he realized that to indulge in further political polemics would be asking for trouble; and so he abandoned the writing of those ephemeral vituperative tracts which had occupied his energies for so long, and returned to his true vocation, that of the poet.

He had long had a vision of producing a great English epic

which would take its place beside the *Iliad* of Homer and the *Aeneid* of Virgil. He never doubted that he could do it, and he pondered long on the choice of subject. The deeds of King Arthur occupied his thoughts for some time, but he finally settled on a theme more ambitious and more sublime: nothing less than the Fall of Man.

Milton had been for most of his life a Londoner, and his final years were spent in the metropolis. His house in the City was burned down in the Great Fire, but subsequently he settled down in Holborn and later in Bunhill, and in these homes he dictated the tremendous epic of *Paradise Lost* to the young pupils who came to him for instruction and who served as his amanuenses.

Paradise Lost was published in 1667, and won swift acclaim. This was not one of those cases of a poet's finest work being left to moulder in obscurity till after the unfortunate author's death; the reading public of Charles II's reign, limited though it was, had sufficient literary taste to recognize the poem for the supreme masterpiece that it was. Splendidly confident in his own powers, Milton, before he started on the epic, had announced his intention of leaving to posterity 'something so written to aftertimes as they should not willingly let it die'; and in a famous line in the poem itself he alluded to 'things unattempted yet in prose or rhyme'. His self-confidence was abundantly justified. The first edition of 1,300 copies was sold out by the time of his death seven years after its publication (high figures in a time of restricted literacy), and in the years that followed new editions were produced at regular intervals. The work received the compliment of imitation. Dryden based an opera on the text, and John Aubrey has a pleasant picture of the younger author courteously calling on the venerable poet and being gravely given permission 'to tagge his verses'. In gratitude Dryden, the acknowledged arbiter of contemporary literary taste, described the epic as 'undoubtedly one of the greatest, most noble, and most sublime poems which either this age or nation has produced'.

Dryden's praise is not exaggerated. As a poem in English on the grand scale *Paradise Lost* stands alone. The story is told in twelve books (in the first form of the poem there were ten), and unfolds in sonorous blank verse which for sustained majesty of language has no equal. It is all in the tradition of *L'Allegro*, *Il Penseroso* and *Lycidas*. Milton's miraculous gift of language was hardly capable of further development after his first fine careless rapture. But the loftiness of the theme and the grandeur of the vision lift *Paradise Lost* above even *Lycidas*. Man in the shape of Adam is the hero of the epic; it could hardly be otherwise in view of Milton's intense religiosity. But he put his greatest poetry into the mouth of the 'villain', the Arch-Fiend Lucifer/Satan, and perhaps subconsciously gave the personification of evil a dignity and a strength of character that dwarfed the images not only of Adam but of all the angels and demons that people the poem, and God himself. The epic is full of political allusions; Milton did not change with the years, and Satan is the supreme rebel against established authority, such as Milton in a Royalist world would have liked himself to be. As such he could not withhold his admiration, which shines forth in all the splendour of his immortal verse. Milton's Satan has been called the greatest character in English literature.

Four years after the publication of *Paradise Lost* came *Paradise Regained*. Sequels are notoriously unrewarding, and the later poem has never received the adulation accorded to the earlier. The subject, the redemption of man through Christ after the loss of Eden, was the natural development of the theme Milton had set himself; one that he had always had in mind. But in the event he restricted himself to the limited horizon of the Temptation of Christ in the Wilderness, and the range of treatment seems small in comparison with the vast panorama of the Fall of Man. Milton's mind, in common with most Puritan thinkers, was more in tune with the Old Testament than the New, and the second epic does not flow with the intellectual ease of the first. Yet the classical background,

always prominent in Milton, is as rich as ever, and the most
notable passages are in the noble descriptions of Athens and
Rome.

In the last of the three great works of his post-Restoration
period, Milton returned to the Old Testament. *Samson Agonistes* saw the fulfilment of his literary life. It is an astonishing
poem, written in a variety of metres, some rhymed and some
not, woven into a verbal harmony which only he could achieve.
All his classical knowledge, all the intensity and individuality
of his Puritan philosophy, find full play in the most auto-
biographical work he ever produced. The blind Samson,
captive of the Philistines, 'eyeless in Gaza, at the mill with
slaves', is the blind Milton isolated in the midst of the religious
and political foes that he hated and despised. The fact that those
foes had treated him with a leniency and magnanimity that he
would never have extended to them was a consideration that
in all probability never occurred to him.

Thus Milton completed his life's work, and awaited his
Nunc dimittis in peace and tranquillity. The fierce puritanism
of his writings was not entirely echoed in his private life:
Aubrey tells us that he was 'of a very cheerfull humour', and
John Phillips that 'his deportment was sweet and affable'. He
enjoyed company, and in his last years was frequently visited
by the leading learned and literary figures of the day who came
to pay their respects to the old master. Apart from the blindness
his health was good until near the end when he was afflicted
with gout. He was sixty-six when he died in 1674.

Closely associated with Milton in more ways than one, but a
very different sort of man, was Andrew Marvell. Thirteen
years younger than his mentor, he served under him in the
Latin Secretariat and maintained a lifelong loyalty to the senior
poet. When Milton, after the Restoration, was attacked in
print by a second-rate writer, Samuel Parker, Marvell came to
his defence in a devastating but reasoned and dignified reply
named *The Rehearsal Transposed* (the allusion in the title is to
Buckingham's comedy *The Rehearsal*).

Marvell, a Yorkshireman, travelled widely in Europe in his youth and imbibed the culture of various nations in addition to their languages; he was an accomplished linguist as well as a classical scholar. For a time during the Commonwealth he lived in Lord Fairfax's great house at Nun Appleton, acting as tutor to the young Mary Fairfax. All these experiences helped to shape the man. Everything in Marvell reflected culture and polish. He became an accomplished politician, but at the same time looked out on life and the world with a faintly amused tolerance. Incapable of rancour or bad temper, he could write the most vigorous satire without displaying malice or acrimony.

Marvell like Milton had his 'Cavalier period'. Some of his early lyrics are among the most charming in the English language: *To his Coy Mistress* ('Had we but World enough, and Time, This coyness Lady were no crime') and *The Gallery* ('Clora come view my Soul, and tell Whether I have contriv'd it well'). And in such poems as *The Garden* ('Fair Quiet, have I found thee here, And Innocence thy Sister dear!') and *The Picture of Little T.C. in a Prospect of Flowers* ('In the green Grass she loves to lie, And there with her fair Aspect tames The Wilder flow'rs, and gives them names') he depicted the beauties of the countryside and the open air in language of unsurpassed delicacy.

His post-Restoration poetry was mainly political and satirical; but through it all his urbanity and good manners, together with deep perceptiveness, persisted. Without being an irreconcilable Republican, he was always in opposition to the court, and he did not hesitate to criticize the King. In *Instructions to a Painter* he held up to ridicule the whole establishment of government and society, from the monarch downwards; and in *The King's Vows* he satirized Charles II's *laissez-faire* attitude by putting into his mouth the lines:

I will have a religion then all of my own,
Where Papist from Protestant shall not be known,

4

But if it grow troublesome I will have none,
I'll wholly abandon all public affairs,
And pass all my time with buffoons and players,
And saunter to Nelly when I should be at prayers.

Marvell was incorruptible, and nothing would compromise his independence. A story is told of him and his sovereign which reveals the man to perfection. King Charles was the last man to resent criticism of himself, and after a particularly severe assault he invited Marvell to an entertainment at Whitehall. The two had a long conversation, and the King was charmed with his visitor's manners and wit. Knowing that the poet was in straitened circumstances, he on the next day sent no less a person than the then Lord Treasurer, the Marquess of Danby, to seek him out at his lodgings. Danby after some difficulty ran him to earth in a small room up a dark staircase in the Strand, and Marvell, astonished at being visited by so eminent a personage, asked if he had not lost his way. Danby, however, assured him that Mr Marvell was the man he was looking for, and presented the King's message, which was simply to ask what His Majesty could do to help him. Marvell was highly amused, and 'replied with his usual pleasantry that kings had it not in their power to serve him; he had no void aching in his breast'. Becoming more serious, he then expressed his great gratitude to the King, but insisted that 'he knew too well the nature of courts to accept of favours, which were expected to bind a man in the chains of their interest'. Danby then said that he hoped that at least the poet would accept the gift of 1,000 guineas which the King had ordered on his behalf; but at this Marvell smiled more than ever, and asserted that he had quite enough for his needs and would not dream of depleting the royal treasury. So minister and poet parted with mutual compliments; 'and Mr. Marvell sent to his bookseller for the loan of one guinea'.

Milton and Marvell were the most eminent poetic survivors of Cromwellian sympathies from the preceding age. On the other side of the fence was Abraham Cowley, as ardent a Royalist, in his writings at least, as ever lived. Actually he was at one time under something of a cloud in the eyes of his fellow-Royalists; for after serving the court and the Queen Mother in a secretarial capacity in France he returned to England and lived quietly in retirement under the Commonwealth regime. It was felt that he made the most of both worlds; but Cowley, a gentle soul, was not cast in the heroic mould and wanted only to be left in peace.

He was ten years younger than Milton, but achieved fame almost as early. The 'marvellous boy' of his generation, he was an established poet when in his teens at Westminster School. His early inspiration—curiously enough, Milton's also —was Spenser; and in later life he recorded how this came about:

> I believe I can tell the particular little chance that filled my head first with such chimes of verse as have never since left ringing there: for I remember when I came to read, and to take some pleasure in it, there was wont to lie in my mother's parlour (I know not by what accident, for she herself never in her life read any book but of devotion), but there was wont to lie Spenser's works. This I happened to fall upon, and was infinitely delighted with the stories of the knights, and giants, and monsters, and brave houses which I found everywhere there (though my understanding had little to do with all this), and by degrees with the tinkling of the rhyme and dance of the numbers; so that I think I had read him all over before I was twelve years old, and was thus made a poet as immediately as a child is made a eunuch.

Thereafter Cowley's fame rapidly increased, and he achieved a renown that has not stood the test of time; in the last years before the Great Civil War it was generally accepted that the two first poets of England were Milton and Cowley, and Cowley had as many admirers as Milton.

Cowley had been greatly influenced by John Donne; he was the most eminent among the followers of that illustrious Jacobean poet to whom Dryden, and later Samuel Johnson, applied the term 'metaphysical'. The 'metaphysicals' were scholarly, sophisticated writers who indulged in fantastic conceits and elaborate metaphors. In Johnson's words, 'the most heterogeneous ideas are yoked violently together; Nature and art are ransacked for illustrations, comparisons, and allusions.'

Cowley, not only a Latinist but a scholar of wide versatility, was the complete metaphysical; at the same time elaboration of his fantasies was tempered by an elegance, a lightness of touch and an underlying humour which made him the most charming of poets. But charm was not quite enough. At the Restoration he was revered by the younger literary generation and accepted (Milton being a remote figure under a political cloud) as the premier poet of the nation and the leader of literary thought. But time showed him to be lacking in the depth of feeling that makes a great poet. In his latter years he produced a religious epic, *Davideis*; it has some splendid lines, but a comparison with *Paradise Lost* reveals its superficiality. Cowley was a fine poet, but deficient in lasting qualities. In the new age he produced little of note.

These three were, in the poetic field, the most distinguished survivors from the previous age. There were, of course, others of lesser note. Sir William Davenant, Poet Laureate and manager of the Duke of York's company of players, continued to turn out poetry of moderate competence and to adapt other men's plays for his theatre in Lincoln's Inn Fields. Davenant, a vain man, was the son, or reputed son, of an Oxford vintner possessed of a lovely wife and a comfortable inn at which Shakespeare was in the habit of staying; the younger William liked to let it be thought that his actual father was the bard, and that he had inherited from him not only his name but his literary talent.

George Wither, Edmund Waller and Sir John Denham were others who had made their names in earlier times. Wither, a

Puritan who had written poetry of high quality in his youth, and Waller, a consistent writer over many decades, both lived to be exceptionally old men for their times, but turned out little of value in their later years. Denham, a court poet, produced after the Restoration a limited output of fine verse, including a memorable tribute to Cowley on the latter's death in 1667. Denham had a chequered career interrupted by bursts of insanity, during one of which, according to Aubrey, he went to King Charles and told him he was the Holy Ghost.

Far away from the literary scene Robert Herrick, that incomparable writer of lyrics, had settled down in a Devon parsonage. He was a reluctant clergyman, but penury had forced him, while still a leading light of the Ben Jonson circle, to accept a living; under the Commonwealth he had been ejected as a Royalist, and he had taken the opportunity to come up to London and get his poems published. But they excited little notice; the times were not propitious. Now he was back in the West Country, contented at last, all passion spent, with an admirable housekeeper and a pet pig, enjoying those rural delights which he had depicted so charmingly while revelling in the fleshpots of London. He wrote no more poetry.

Another poet who stood rather apart from his contemporaries was Samuel Butler. His fame rests on one poem, the lengthy *Hudibras*. This immortal mock-epic, composed in octosyllabic couplets, was a ferocious but hilarious attack on Puritans and Puritan hypocrisy. The shafts of ridicule which Butler directed at his Presbyterian squire, 'Sir Hudibras', and his associates were unsurpassed even by Dryden. The poem was mostly written during the last days of the Commonwealth, but Butler not unnaturally had to wait for better times before publication could be considered. His fame in consequence dates from the early years of the Restoration.

English prose in the seventeenth century followed a rather different course from that of poetry. Literature in general, in those medieval days when the bulk of the population was illiterate, had been the province of learned men; and learned men, since learning was international to an extent that it has never been again, had tended to write in the international language, Latin. But poetry by its nature strains against confinement, and budding poets found Latin too constrictive for their art. Great poetry had blossomed in the ancient world, but poets in the Middle Ages, as always, were in search of something new and were not to be satisfied with imitations of Virgil, Horace or Ovid. And so a body of verse, largely forgotten today but of considerable merit, came to be produced in what is now known as 'Middle English'. The writers were mainly ecclesiastics, since only the clergy were sufficiently educated, but the subject-matter was by no means confined to religion.

This literature reached its flowering—and a splendid flowering it was—in the fourteenth century. Robert Mannyng, Richard Rolle and others, chroniclers and preachers in verse, led up to Langland and Chaucer. Geoffrey Chaucer, England's first great poet and certainly one of the three or four greatest who have ever written in English, came rather at the end of a literary epoch than at the beginning; he was the heir of the Middle English poets of the twelfth and thirteenth centuries, and with him the language reached its culmination and its perfection. After him there was a decline; little English verse of quality was produced in the fifteenth century. But when the revival came, in the Tudor age, English poetry rose again as a fully developed vehicle of thought and expression. There would be changes of form in the future, but Shakespeare and his contemporaries knew all that was needed to know about the expression of ideas in verse.

In prose, however, the classics continued for a longer period to hold sway. Latin remained the language considered suitable for philosophical and theological writing, while legal documents employed a curious mixture of Latin, English and Norman French. Yet all the time, from the age of Chaucer onwards, a genuine English prose was gradually evolving. Chaucer himself wrote fluently and lucidly in the vernacular, but in this as in other forms of literature he was in advance of his time. His successors for a century and more wrote in a style that for their contemporaries, as for posterity, can never have been easy to read. It was an English struggling to free itself of bondage to classical tongues, full of Latin constructions, of elaborate sentences, fantastic conceits and far-fetched metaphors. At its best it reached heights of sonorous beauty, and it found its culmination in the superb prose of the Authorized Version of the Bible, the work of a group of the most eminent Anglican theologians of the day, published under the authority of King James I in 1611.

All this developing prose of the fifteenth and sixteenth centuries, however, even the Authorized Version itself, was devised for the edification of the cultural élite. With the growth of literacy among the general population a simpler type of writing was needed, and during the seventeenth century this was gradually achieved.

The paramount influence was the Great Civil War. All wars produce a mass of propaganda, each side striving to impress upon the rank and file the justice of its cause. And in this particular war, in which both sides were English, both aimed at a more direct English in which to appeal to the mass of English-men. Much of the literature produced was of course trash, at the best ephemeral; but it had its effect on the language none the less. Preachers thundered their anathemas, proving from scripture that God was on their side. Pamphleteers poured forth their polemics, denouncing and ridiculing their opponents. And the newspaper industry came into its own.

Newspapers evolved from the news bulletins and news letters that diplomats and politicians employed agents to write to them, describing events at home when they themselves were abroad. These developed into occasional published news-sheets or 'Corantos' in the early years of Charles I. But the general publication of weekly and bi-weekly 'newsbooks' began with the Civil War. Both sides produced them; some lasted only a few weeks, but a few, such as the Parliamentarians'

Mercurius Britannicus and the Royalists' *Mercurius Aulicus*, were of more than ephemeral interest. The editor of *Mercurius Aulicus* was the formidable Sir John Birkenhead, whom Dame Veronica Wedgwood has called 'the true father of English journalism'. He presented his news in concise and readable form, calculated to appeal to any literate observer; and his skill in ridiculing the rival propaganda of the Roundheads gave his journal a wide circulation.

There was thus in being at the time of the Restoration a new style of writing, aiming at lucidity rather than extravagance of language, a popular rather than an aristocratic form of expression. All it needed now was its adoption by writers of the first water who would give it the polish that most of the Civil War literature had lacked.

There were of course some who maintained the old elaborate style. Milton continued to write prose after 1660; his style was always dignified, but his sentences were tortuous and his classical allusions all-pervading and sometimes obscure. He remained one of the old school.

A greater prose writer was Sir Thomas Browne, the Norwich physician, author of *Religio Medici* and *Urn Burial*. Browne, an attractive character, was born two years after the accession of James I and died three years before Charles II. He lived all his life in Norwich, intent on science, religion and philosophy, managing to keep himself remote from the public events of his time. When King and Parliament were at each other's throats he propounded his meditations on the religion of a doctor. When the English monarchy was at its last gasp he published his treatise on *Vulgar Errors*. In the precarious days that led up to the Restoration he discussed the burial customs of antiquity. In none of his writings is there any hint that the times were out of joint.

Browne's writing is the quintessence of the old style; yet his sonorous sentences, fraught with classical learning and packed with words coined from Latin and Greek originals, have a felicity that few prose writers have ever achieved. A random reading of his books never fails to light upon phrases that live in the memory: 'But the quincunx of heaven runs low, and 'tis time to close the five ports of knowledge'; 'Half our days we pass in the shadow of the earth; and the brother of death exacteth a third part of our lives'; 'The Aegyptian Mummies, which Cambyses or time hath spared, avarice now consumeth'.

Browne's style, like that of many of his predecessors and contemporaries, was closely akin to poetry; and from one point of view the change that came over English prose writing from the time of the Civil War onwards may be regarded as a freeing of the convention from poetic shackles. One who typified this state of transition was Edward Hyde Earl of Clarendon.

Charles II's great Lord Chancellor was one of the supreme prose writers of the English language. His *History of the Great Rebellion*, the fusion of two separate manuscripts, begun in the dark days of the interregnum and completed in his second exile after 1667, stood alone as a work of literary historical writing until the publication of Macaulay's unfinished *History of England* nearly two centuries later. Clarendon's accomplishment as a statesman in securing the smooth passage of the Restoration, and in guiding the progress of the reinstated monarchy, was great and enduring; but his prime claim to immortality rests on the *History of the Great Rebellion*.

It would be wholly wrong to describe the style of this tremendous work as poetic. It is a lawyer's English, lucid and businesslike. Yet at the same time Clarendon's orotund phrases, his elaborately compiled sentences, belong to an older tradition. As a historian he is not always reliable; he was careless about dates, and his personal prejudices are omnipresent. But as a descriptive writer, and as a delineator of character, he was unsurpassed.

He was not, however, typical of his age. It would be a mistake to regard Restoration prose as marking too abrupt a break from past tradition; but the prose of Charles II's reign in general bears a new and more colloquial character, born of the troubles of the previous age, the growth of literacy, and the approach to a more catholic readership.

One of the pioneers was Cowley, whose essays, dating from the early years of the Restoration, were written in an easy, artless, almost conversational style, in marked contrast with the formal manner of earlier essay-writers such as Bacon. Cowley's essays, however, were few in number and small in content. In so far as the new development was a movement, and as a movement could boast of a leader, that leader was the epitome of Restoration culture, John Dryden.

From time to time in the evolution of English literature there arises a towering figure who dominates the age by means both of his talent and his personality, and who by example, criticism and sheer force of character influences his contemporaries to such an extent that their writings are inevitably related to his own standards and judgements. Such in the Jacobean age, in spite of the superior quality of Shakespeare, was Ben Jonson. Such in the eighteenth century was Jonson's almost-namesake, Samuel Johnson. Such in recent times, in a slightly different manner, was Bernard Shaw. And such in the Restoration era was Dryden.

In the eyes of most literary critics Dryden's fame rests on his verse. But his prose was of at least equal importance. He it was who brought to perfection the easy, semi-colloquial style of Cowley and added to it an elegance, a balance and a dignity that were all his own. His style was the essence of the seventeenth-century conception of 'wit'. In the words of Dame Veronica Wedgwood, 'he gave to English prose the note of an easy and well-bred familiarity, and showed by his example that written English could *appear* as spontaneous as spoken, although in reality concealing a consummate artistry in the balancing of the sentence, the introduction of metaphor, the breaking and alternation of rhythm.'

Dryden was an urbane Londoner. Everything he wrote was sane, balanced and judicious. 'Polite' is the adjective most often applied to his work; his irony was biting but always restrained and controlled. Passion and excessive emotion were alien to his spirit. His literary activities spanned almost the whole of the second half of the seventeenth century; he was born in 1631, and he first came into prominence in 1659 with a poem in commemoration of Oliver Cromwell. Dryden was then twenty-eight, and he went on writing almost till his death in 1700.

In both prose and verse he concerned himself with the public affairs of the day, political and religious. He has been accused of being a time-server, starting as he did as a praiser of the Cromwellian regime and quickly switching to support of King Charles with his *Astraea Redux* acclaiming the Restoration. But Dryden had reached years of discretion under the shadow of the Protectorate, and as an upholder of law and concord he tended from his youth onwards to support the established order. A monarchical society was his natural orbit, as he quickly came to realize. 'Both my nature, as I am an Englishman,' he wrote in a characteristic passage, 'and my reason, as I am a man, have bred in me a loathing to that specious name of a republick: that mock appearance of a liberty, where all who have not part in the government are slaves; and slaves they are of a viler note than such as are subjects to an absolute dominion.' At the same time there were limits to his subservience to authority, and he never violated his conscience. When William III came to power he resigned the Laureateship rather than renounce his recent conversion to Catholicism.

In his prose writings Dryden was most highly esteemed for his literary criticism. And indeed there has seldom been a finer critic. He was at once acute and generous; his contemporaries hung on his words and vied with each other for his praise. He was equally judicious in his estimates of past writers. He, if anybody, established the supremacy of Shakespeare in an age in which Jonson, the more forceful character, was still more widely admired. Referring to Jonson, Dryden wrote: 'If I would compare him with Shakespeare, I must acknowledge him the more correct poet, but Shakespeare the greater wit. Shakespeare was the Homer, or father of our dramatic poets; Jonson was the Virgil, the pattern of elaborate writing; I admire him, but I love Shakespeare.'

Dryden was a master of the evocative phrase, always produced in the most effective context. In his essay *Of Dramatic Poesy* he described how, in an imaginary (or perhaps a real) trip on the Thames in the first summer of the Second Dutch War, when the guns of the Battle of Lowestoft were audible in London, four friends fell to discussing the respective merits of ancient and modern, and of French and English, dramatists. The four, portrayed under classical pseudonyms, are generally agreed to have been Sir Robert Howard, Lord Buckhurst, Sir Charles Sedley and Dryden himself. Lounging comfortably in their barge, they covered the whole field of theatrical literature, and in the dialogue, a favourite device of the time, Dryden's considered views on the subject came into play. At last in the cool of the evening, while still deep in discourse, the four found themselves back at Somerset Stairs, where they were to land.

. . . The company were all sorry to separate so soon, though a great part of the evening was already spent; and stood a-while looking back on the water, upon which the moon-beams played, and made it appear like floating quicksilver; at last they went up through a crowd of French people, who were merrily dancing in the open air, and nothing concerned for the noise of guns which had alarmed the town that afternoon . . .

As in prose, so in verse, Dryden's was the pre-eminent name among Restoration writers. He was entirely of his age; wit was the essence of his poetry; elegance and good manners characterized its form. He wrote quickly and easily and was immensely prolific. Plays, elegies, satires, translations, poured from his pen over a period of nearly half a century. He translated the *Aeneid* and adapted Shakespeare; he wrote both tragedies and comedies; he commemorated public events such as King

Charles's coronation and battles at sea; he described brilliantly such disasters as the Great Plague and the Fire of London. He was master of all forms of verse; adept at rhymed couplets in his early days, turning to blank verse in his best-known tragedy, *All for Love* (on the subject of Antony and Cleopatra, frankly adapted from Shakespeare but written in a very different manner). His *Annus Mirabilis* of 1666 is written in rhymed quatrains, and in his later *Song for St Cecilia's Day* and *Alexander's Feast* he experimented with rhythmic metres of his own, designed to be set to music.

He is best remembered now for his satire. Such brilliant ridicule, always under the guise of good temper, has seldom been cast on contemporaries by a poet as in *Absalom and Achitophel*, *The Medall* and *MacFlecknoe*. In the first of these he defended his King against Shaftesbury and his cronies who were conspiring to alter the succession. In the last he turned on his fellow-poet Thomas Shadwell, a rough, heavy man who had set himself up as a rival to Dryden and who eventually superseded him as Poet Laureate:

> The rest to some faint meaning make pretense,
> But *Shadwell* never deviates into sense.
> Some Beams of wit on other souls may fall,
> Strike through and make a lucid intervall;
> But *Shadwell*'s genuine night admits no ray,
> His rising fogs prevail upon the Day:
> Besides, his goodly Fabrick fills the eye
> And seems design'd for thoughtless Majesty:
> Thoughtless as Monarch Oakes that shade the plain,
> And, spread in solemn state, supinely reign.

Dryden became Poet Laureate after the death of Davenant in 1668. Thereafter his influence was even greater than before. His natural authority was enhanced by official recognition. This was the age of the coffee-houses, ancestors of modern London clubs, where beverages other than coffee were provided but where polite conversation ruled in contrast with the brawling conditions of the older taverns. Dryden's name is indelibly associated with Will's Coffee House in Covent Garden. Here he was in his element, having his own accustomed chair which by universal consent was accorded to him; and here for some thirty years he dispensed words of urbane wisdom and listened with kindly ear to the aspirations of budding poets who sat at his feet as the 'Tribe of Ben' had sat at the feet of Jonson in more boisterous conditions half a century before.

Dryden was bitterly attacked in his lifetime by envious rivals, and at least once he was the victim of a brutal physical assault. But he was a gentle man, generous to his friends and magnanimous in his judgements. As a writer he has been much underrated since his death. Critics have portrayed him as stilted and uninspired, an unimaginative precursor of the Augustan Age. He was far more than that. By his own talent and cultural qualities he shaped the entire literature of a generation, and he brought the English language to a technical perfection which it had never attained before. It may be doubted whether it has been improved upon since.

The lesser planets of Restoration literature circled round the sun that was Dryden. In whatever they attempted he excelled them. Nevertheless they made a vital contribution to the culture of the age, for if they did nothing else they made writing a fashionable activity. A little clique of aristocrats, who included Sir George Etherege, Sir Charles Sedley, Charles Sackville Lord Buckhurst (later Earl of Dorset), the Earl of Rochester, and even the Duke of Buckingham, did more than dabble in literature; they produced a quantity of poems and plays which were on the whole of secondary quality but contained an element of value. They were rakes first and authors second; most of them lived lives of riotous debauchery, and their object was to shock the Puritans and philistines both by their behaviour and by their writings. They drank and gambled their time away; they fought in the streets and attacked the watch; and their lives were intermingled with those of

London's most celebrated harlots. They celebrated their peccadilloes without shame in prose and verse. Buckhurst gravely thanked the famous Moll Hinton for giving him the pox, 'a greater favour than any of your sex have bestowed on me this five year'.

In the eyes of Rochester, the most acute literary critic of the day after Dryden, Buckhurst was 'the best good man, with the worst natur'd muse'. The same critic said of Sedley:

> For Songs and Verses, mannerly, obscene,
> That can stir Nature up by spring unseen,
> And without forcing blushes please the Queen,
> Sedley has that prevailing, gentle Art,
> That can with a resistless Charm impart,
> The loosest Wishes to the chastest Heart,
> Raise such a Conflict, kindle such a Fire
> Betwixt declining Vertue and Desire;
> Till the poor vanquish'd Mind dissolves away,
> In Dreames all Night, in Sighs and Tears all Day.

This was the prime aim of the Restoration poets, and the majority of their songs and verses celebrated the joys of love and the conquest of mistresses. Sedley was one of the best of them, and some of his lyrics have a charm all their own:

> Phillis is my only Joy,
> Faithless as the Winds or Seas;
> Sometimes coming, sometimes coy,
> Yet she never fails to please;
>   If with a Frown
>   I am cast down,
>   Phillis smiling,
>   And beguiling,
> Makes me happier than before.
> Tho', alas, too late I find,
> Nothing can her Fancy fix;

Yet the Moment she is kind,
I forgive her all her Tricks;
    Which, tho I see,
    I can't get free;
    She deceiving
    I believing;
What need Lovers wish for more?

In a more direct tribute to a lady, coupled with his other chief
joy in life, Sedley wrote:

Her lips are two brimmers of claret,
Where first I began to miscarry;
    Her breasts of delight
    Are two bottles of white
And her eyes are two cups of canary.

Etherege and Buckhurst wrote poetry of a similar kind but
usually in a coarser and less good-tempered key. They wrote
rather on the pains than on the joys of love; like many habitual
womanizers they had savage thoughts about the sex that gave
them pleasure. Thus Etherege:

And here and there I had her,
And everywhere I had her,
Her toy was such that every touch
Would make a lover madder.

For he that would have a wench kind
Ne'er smugs up himself like a ninny,
But plainly tells her his mind
And tickles her first with a guinea.

And Buckhurst, in whose family there was a strong literary
tradition:

Dorinda's sparkling wit, and eyes
United, cast too fierce a light,
Which blazes high, but quickly dies,
Pains not the heart, but hurts the sight.

Love is a calmer, gentler joy,
 Smooth are his looks, and soft his pace;
Her Cupid is a black-guard boy,
 That runs his link full in your face.

Reading these light amorous verses constantly induces the thought that, in this branch of literature as in almost all others of the time, the pupils were excelled by the master. 'Dryden in vain try'd this nice way of wit,' wrote Rochester, ' . . . and thus he got the name of Poet Squab.' But in fact when Dryden did try he produced lyrics that put others to shame. Nothing could be lighter or more charming than his vision of a youthful seduction in the countryside:

Sylvia the fair, in the bloom of fifteen,
Felt an innocent warmth as she lay on the green;
She had heard of a pleasure and something she guessed
By the tumbling and touzing and touching her breast;
She saw the men eager, but was at a loss
What they meant by their sighing and kissing so close,
 By their praying and whining
 And clasping and twining
 And panting and wishing
 And sighing and kissing
 And sighing and kissing so close.

'Ah,' she cried, 'ah, for a languishing maid
In a country of Christians to die without aid!
Not a Whig, or a Tory, or Trimmer at least,
Or Protestant parson or Catholic priest,
To instruct a young virgin that is at a loss
What they mean by their sighing and kissing so close!

By their praying and whining
And clasping and twining
And panting and wishing
And sighing and kissing
And sighing and kissing so close.'

Cupid in shape of a swain did appear;
He saw the sad wound and in pity drew near,
Then showed her his arrow and bade her not fear,
For the pain was no more than a maiden might bear.
When the balm was infused she was not at a loss
What they meant by their sighing and kissing so close,
　　By their praying and whining
　　And clasping and twining
　　And panting and wishing
　　And sighing and kissing
　　And sighing and kissing so close.

The only writer among that gay and gallant company of poetasters who could really challenge comparison with Dryden, though in fact he came rather late on the Restoration scene, was John Wilmot Earl of Rochester. This brilliant, dissolute, unstable young man was the son of Henry Wilmot, the joyous, carefree Cavalier who had fought for Charles I, fallen foul of him, and then shared the younger Charles's adventures after the Battle of Worcester. In the years of exile Charles II continued his friendship with Henry and created him Earl of Rochester.

The second Earl had much of his father in him, his reckless disposition and his independence of spirit; but he was of much greater intellect and even wilder in his conduct. He was the spoilt darling of Charles II's court; the King, who had been devoted to the elder Wilmot, continued his favour to the younger, who repaid his kindness by lampooning him in lines that would have met with the direst consequences from a less tolerant monarch. He wrote of his sovereign:

Restless he rolls about from whore to whore,
A merry monarch, scandalous and poor.
Nor are his high desires above his strength;
His sceptre and his ———— are of a length.

Rochester was given almost unbelievable licence at court. His
debaucheries were a byword; he was known in every brothel
in London; and he was as violent as he was vicious. He fought
duels and brawled in the streets. He was undoubtedly responsible for the savage attack made by bravos on Dryden in
Rose Alley after a literary squabble in 1679.

At the same time he wrote some of the finest poetry produced
in his time. Much of his verse was scurrilous, much of it obscene;
it frequently contained four-letter words (in most cases not
spelt out in the text) which have prevented its reprinting until
recent times. But he was a satirist of brilliant force, a critic of
sense and judgement, and a lyric poet of high talent. In between
his bouts of violence and drunkenness he acted as a generous
patron of writers less well off than himself.

Rochester was not all rake. There was another side of his
character that showed itself from time to time. He was subject
not only to outbursts of dissipation but to equally strong fits
of genuine remorse; deep in his heart he was a religious man,
and when he died, worn out by his excesses, at the age of
thirty-two, his deathbed was one of Christian penitence. Above
all, he had a real devotion to his wife, the heiress Elizabeth
Malet whom he had abducted at the age of eighteen. After all
his endless infidelities he always went back to her, the one
stable refuge of his wandering life; and he expressed his feelings
for her in one of his best-known lyrics:

Absent from thee I languish still;
    Then ask me not, When I return?
The straying Fool 'twill plainly kill,
    To wish all Day, all Night to mourn.

Dear; from thine Arms then let me fly,
  That my fantastick Mind may prove,
The Torments it deserves to try,
  That tears my fixt Heart from my Love.

When wearied with a World of Woe,
  To thy safe Bosom I retire,
Where Love and Peace and Truth does flow,
  May I contented there expire.

Lest once more wand'ring from that Heav'n,
  I fall on some base Heart unblest;
Faithless to thee, false, unforgiven,
  And lose my everlasting Rest.

Yet in another mood he could write:

Of all the Bedlams marriage is the worst,
With endless cords, with endless keepers curst!
Frantic in love you run, and rave about,
Mad to get in, but hopeless to get out.

Rochester had the makings of a greater poet than he ever
became. As it was his fame rests, as does that of Byron and
Wilde in later ages, more on the manner of his life than on
what he wrote.

It was in the theatre that the talents of the Restoration wits
found their most prolific output. It was their natural element,
for under the aegis of the King and the Duke of York the
theatre soon became the centre of fashionable life. The King's
House under Killigrew, which had two or three successive
sites, was finally established in Drury Lane; and the Duke's
House under Davenant, after a period in Lincoln's Inn, in
Salisbury Court.

The establishment of the Restoration theatre was part of a
continuous development. The Civil War had, as in most

aspects of life, marked the end of an epoch; but there was no complete break with the theatre of Shakespeare and Jonson. Stage production was never wholly obliterated under the Commonwealth. Plays continued to be performed, at first clandestinely but gradually more openly. When King Charles returned there were several theatres operating in London.

The Restoration stage, however, did differ in certain essentials from that of earlier days. Killigrew, Davenant and their associates had been among the Royalist exiles and had grown accustomed to the Paris theatre of the early days of Louis XIV, a theatre more cultured, elegant and highly developed than anything London could boast. These developments they now introduced into the new playhouses. Closed buildings (they started in covered-in converted tennis courts) provided a more intimate atmosphere than the old open-air arenas, and a proscenium arch with curtain, footlights and painted scenery took the place of the Elizabethan bare and open stage, now to be banished for three centuries before its return to popularity in our own times.

A far more important development was the appearance of actresses. In the Elizabethan-Jacobean theatre women's parts had all been taken by boys or young men. The medieval prejudice against women on the stage still prevailed; where professional actresses existed (and they began to appear on Continental stages long before they were allowed in London) it was taken for granted that they were prostitutes, as in fact a great many of them were. An actress appearing in public in the London of pre-Civil-War days would have been in danger of being mobbed, and quite possibly lynched, by puritanical bully-boys.

In amateur and more sophisticated circles, indeed, women performers did appear—from the highest in the land downwards. Both Anne of Denmark and Henrietta Maria loved to take part in the masques that were such features of court life in the reigns of James I and Charles I, and of course the ladies of the royal retinue followed suit. But the opposition was vitriolic. The fanatical William Prynne in his *Histriomastix*, a gigantic work of interminable vituperation, castigated Queen Henrietta with such fury as to bring him a stretch in the pillory, a £5,000 fine, perpetual imprisonment (it was not in fact perpetual) and the loss of his ears.

When professional actresses took their proper place on the London stage, as they did immediately after the Restoration, the custom was, like so many aspects of Carolean culture, an importation from France. The boy 'actresses' of former days disappeared; such of them as were still in the profession, such as Edward Kynaston, were now grown up and played men's parts, and there were no new recruits. There were plenty of fine actors on the Restoration stage. Foremost among them was Thomas Betterton, one of the half-dozen or so masculine players to be acknowledged as among the greatest of their profession in English history—to be equalled, perhaps, only by Garrick, Kean and Irving. Charles Hart, Michael Mohun and Will Mountford were others who shone on the boards.

But it was the actresses who caught the eye. They were the new element, welcome and ornamental, and they played a vital part in the Restoration scene that was not limited to the stage. It is uncertain who was the first of them, but the honour seems to belong to Ann Marshall. She was quickly followed by Margaret Hughes, who was in due course to become the mistress of Prince Rupert. Others were Katherine Corey, Anne Gibbs, Hester Davenport and Ann Marshall's sister Rebecca; the crude Betty Mackerel and the respectable Mary Saunderson, wife of Thomas Betterton. A little later came Elizabeth Barry, who was credited with a host of lovers; and the most famous of all, Nell Gwyn, who after living with Charles Hart and Charles Lord Buckhurst settled down to adorn the bed of her 'Charles the Third', the King of Great Britain himself.

Round these charming ladies the world of the Restoration wits revolved. They flitted from bed to bed, and there were few who could not boast a literary lover or two. And in return for services rendered, the talented young men turned out plays in which their favourites could shine. Thus the worlds of the court, of the theatre and of literature merged with one another. Killigrew and Betterton themselves wrote plays; Lady Castlemaine included a rope-dancer among her lovers; the Duke of Buckingham turned playwright; and the King was as much at home in the green-room as in Whitehall.

It was in this elegant, sophisticated, somewhat raffish atmosphere that Restoration comedy came to fruition. It was not quite a new creation. Cowley's *Cutter of Coleman Street*, written before the Restoration though later remodelled, was in the form, though hardly the spirit, of the later plays. But Restoration comedy, as the term is generally understood, belongs entirely to the reigns of Charles II and his immediate successors. Its essential ingredients are wit, urbanity and sophistication. Its appeal is to the head; never to the heart. The scene is almost invariably London—its streets, parks and coffee houses. The themes are, almost exclusively, love, sexual intrigue and cuckoldry.

The convention was largely founded on Molière. Dryden, inevitably, was one of the first in the field. *The Wild Gallant*, *Sir Martin Mar-All* and *Marriage à la Mode* set the fashion; but this was not Dryden's favourite medium and he soon lost interest, preferring to write tragedy. Etherege was another pioneer; he had been schooled in France, and his plays owed a direct debt to Molière. His first, *The Comical Revenge*, is written partly in prose, partly in rhymed couplets. Later writers abandoned verse, except for occasional songs interpolated in the text. Etherege was followed by Sedley, whose *The Mulberry Garden* showed a considerable advance. Buckingham in *The Rehearsal* produced a clever satire on Dryden, though how far the play was really his is uncertain.

These playwrights were put in the shade by William Wycherley, who had also been trained in France. His comedies were more sexually outrageous than anything that had gone before; and the Restoration audience loved them. He reached his zenith in *The Country Wife*, the hero of which, Horner, is enabled to enjoy the favours of his friends' wives through posing

as a eunuch. But Wycherley was more than just a salaciou
dramatist out to shock. He brought a sharp wit and grea
industry to the writing of his well-constructed plays. Rocheste
wrote of him:

> But Wicherley earns hard what e'er he gains,
> He wants no judgements, and he spares no pains;
> He frequently excells, and at the least,
> Makes fewer faults than any of the best.

Rochester himself, who was the lover of Elizabeth Barry among
others, did not go in seriously for play-writing, though he tried
his hand at it. But a close friend of his, Aphra Behn, who may o
may not have been one of his mistresses, wrote some of the
best comedies of the epoch.

Aphra Behn was a writer to whom, at least until recent years,
inadequate justice has been done. Women were rare phenomena
in the English literary scene before the nineteenth century, but
the Restoration era could boast two of considerable talent,
Katherine Philips and Aphra Behn. Mrs Philips, born in the
same year as Dryden, was a bluestocking, the centre of a rarefied
literary group on the Welsh border which included the poet
Henry Vaughan. She translated Corneille into English and
composed high-souled poems on friendship to her beloved
neighbour Anne Owen; in the fashion of the times she called
herself Orinda and her friend Lucasia.

Mrs Behn was of a different type. Her husband, of whom
little is known, was Dutch or German; he died soon after they
were married, and Aphra throughout her life had to live,
literally, by her wits. In her young days she lived in South
America and in the Netherlands, and at the time of the Second
Dutch War she was employed on secret service work at Antwerp
by Charles II. A little later she found herself in prison for debt.
Then she turned to literature, churning out prose and verse,
drama and fiction, with a facility equal to that of any of her male
rivals and holding her own with the best of them. She was the

first Englishwoman to make a success of authorship as a regular profession.

This early champion of women's rights was a genuine poet; the best of her verse could bear comparison with the works of Dryden, who admired and encouraged her. In her comedies she set herself undisguisedly to shock the Puritans, to produce plays that should rival any written by her masculine contemporaries for salacity and sexual candour. In this she succeeded admirably. Such plays of hers as *The Amorous Prince, The Dutch Lover, The Town Fop* and *Sir Patient Fancy* were, both for wit and explicitness, worthy of Wycherley.

It was her very success that ruined her reputation in later ages. Jealous rivals in her own time, furious at feminine intrusion into masculine preserves, assiduously spread gossip about her private life which was assumed to be on a par with the licence displayed in her plays. Her latest biographer, Miss Maureen Duffy, considers this reputation unjustified; Aphra, she thinks, had only one real love affair in her life. Be this as it may, she was branded as 'a literary harlot', and this did her damage with posterity. At the time she gave as good as she got, supported as she was by such critics as Dryden and Rochester. But the more prissy centuries that followed the Restoration era shunned her plays and held up hands of horror at the supposed lasciviousness of her life. Thus to this day she has not been given her due.

Aphra Behn wrote tragedy as well as comedy, but tragedy was not her *forte*; nor was it the *forte* of the age in which she wrote. Restoration tragedy, written mostly in blank verse or rhymed couplets, was imitative, founded mainly on Racine. Its finest flower, Dryden's *All for Love*, contains magnificent lines but is stilted and lifeless compared with the Shakespearean master-piece on which it was founded.

There was, however, another branch of literature in which a real advance was made in the reign of Charles II; and here again the name of Aphra Behn is pre-eminent. This was the novel. The origins of the English novel are a matter of dispute. The old idea that it began with Defoe and Richardson is now discounted. It went back at least to Lyly and Greene in Elizabethan days; and what is Chaucer's *Tale of Melibeus* if not a novel?

There was a distinct step forward in Restoration days. *The English Rogue* by Richard Head, a long piece of semi-pornographic fiction interspersed with innumerable sub-plots (or novels within a novel) tells the story of a disreputable vagabond and his criminal and sexual adventures. But Aphra Behn's fiction is both tidier and more akin to the novel as it is known today. It is true that her prose works are brief, and could properly be described as short stories. But they have both plot and pattern. The most famous of them, *Oroonoko*, certainly her prose masterpiece, recounts the tragic life history of a West African prince sold into slavery at Surinam in South America, where Aphra had herself spent some of her early years. The story was almost certainly based on fact; but it is a genuine work of fiction.

Finally, in this brief survey of Restoration literature, some mention must be made of the underground pornography which circulated so freely and much of which has in recent years found its way into print. This form of writing has flourished in most eras, and in content many of the manuscripts which have come to light do not differ greatly from such romances as *Two Schoolgirls in Paris* and *The Autobiography of a Flea* which titillated the sexual palates of Victorian and later connoisseurs. But there was perhaps an exceptional amount of this type of writing in the time of Charles II. The age was free from hypocrisy, and its literary licence provided plenty of published work to satisfy most patrons of pornography. But there was a quantity of anonymous material in manuscript form that passed clandestinely from hand to hand. Much of it consisted of satirical verse on the gentlemen, and more particularly the ladies, of the royal circle, and a great deal of it was certainly written by courtiers and fashionable writers, such as Sedley and Buckhurst, who were closely in touch with the facts they purported to record.

It was the participation of such wits as these that gave this underground literature what distinction it can boast. Above all there was Rochester. A great deal of his published work was sufficiently obscene to satisfy the most demanding taste, but he undoubtedly contributed also to the underground market. It is difficult to be precise, for any pornographic verse that showed a trace of wit was almost automatically credited to the licentious earl. There is in the British Museum the manuscript of a play called *Sodom or the Quintessence of Debauchery* which is specifically attributed to Rochester; it deals in explicit detail with the orgies, both homosexual and heterosexual, at the court of King Bolloxinion of Sodom. But critical scholars doubt if the attribution is correct.

The most famous pornographic poem of the period, however, was also attributed to Rochester, and though later hands probably contributed to it the original version seems to have been written by him. It is called *Signior Dildo* and describes how the personification of that aid to sexual satisfaction came to England in the train of Mary of Modena, second wife of James Duke of York. A few verses will suffice to give an example of the type of underground literature popular at the court of Charles II:

You ladies all of merry England
Who have been to kiss the Duchess's hand,
Pray, did you lately observe in the show
A noble Italian called Signior Dildo?

The Signior was one of her Highness's train
And helped to conduct her over the main,
But now she cried out, 'To the Duke I will go;
I have no more need for Signior Dildo' . . .

You'll take him at first for no person of note,
Because he appears in a plain leather coat,
But when you his virtuous abilities know,
You'll fall down and worship Signior Dildo.

That pattern of virtue, her Grace of Cleveland,
Has swallowed more pricks than the nation has land;
But by rubbing and scrubbing so large it does grow
It is fit for just nothing but Signior Dildo.

Our dainty fine duchesses have got a trick
To dote on a fool for the sake of his prick;
The fops were undone did their graces but know
The discretion and vigour of Signior Dildo . . .

Doll Howard no more with his Highness must range,
And therefore is proffered this civil exchange:
Her teeth being rotten, she smells best below,
And needs must be fitted for Signior Dildo . . .

There are many other poems of a similar nature, equally crud
but less witty and more ill-natured. They are of little importanc
in the context of Restoration literature, but are not withou
interest as throwing light on the life and morals of the court o
King Charles II.

The Mind and the Senses

Mean while the Mind, from pleasure less,
Withdraws into its happiness:
The Mind, that Ocean where each kind
Does streight its own resemblance find;
Yet it creates, transcending these,
Far other Worlds, and other Seas;
Annihilating all that's made
To a green Thought in a green Shade.

Andrew Marvell

The bounds of human knowledge are constantly being extended. Much of the learning of the ancient world was indeed lost to western civilization when the barbarian invasions put an end to the Roman Empire and the old culture was forced underground; but in the Middle Ages the Catholic Church, and in particular its monasteries, laboriously built up a new body of scholarship, theological in its direction but universal in its application, founded on the study of the universal language, Latin. It was the peculiar glory of the fifteenth-century Renaissance, apart from its pre-eminence in the visual arts, that it rediscovered the treasures, intellectual and artistic, of Greek and Roman civilization. Hence the name given to the scholars of the period, *Humanists*, students of the art and literature of the ancient world, with their revelations of the nature of humanity and the human race which had become obscured in the study of the divine that had monopolized the studies of the medieval schoolmen.

In the years that followed the range of learning was immeasurably widened. The Humanists had concentrated on the study of Greek, neglected in the obsession of the Middle Ages with Latin, and therein opened up fields of study long obscured. Plato and Aristotle, Herodotus and Thucydides, Sophocles and

Aristophanes, Praxiteles and Zeuxis, came back into their ow
In the next age a new attention to the vernacular tongu
developed into a general study of the age in which men no
lived. The explorations of the fifteenth and sixteenth centuri
brought knowledge of distant lands which had hitherto bee
legendary. And the natural sciences emerged from the shackl
of myth and magic.

The seventeenth century played its essential part in th
extension of human knowledge. Like all ages it was one
transition, not noticeably different in kind from those tha
preceded and followed it. It was characterized by intens
scientific activity and curiosity, and also by the interest taken i
philosophy and science by an impressive number of monarch
and magnates who in a hierarchical age lent their support an
patronage to the work of scholars and artists.

It was also, in England as elsewhere, an age of intellectu
versatility; an era, perhaps the last, in which it was still
possible, for all the constant expansion of learning, for
scholar to take all human knowledge for his province. Franci
Bacon, the father of modern English philosophy, had don
something very near to this; and so did some of his successor
at the time of the Restoration. The cult of finding out more an
more about less and less lay in the future; the ideal of univers
learning was not beyond the horizon of the individual scholar.

England played a full part in the intellectual activity of th
century. English *savants* had from the beginning held their ow
with their compeers on the Continent, and inspiration was give
to their efforts by the pre-eminent work of Bacon. The restora
tion of the monarchy supplied a new impetus. The country'
Puritan rulers were by no means devoid of intellectual ability
but the years 1640–1660 were a time of action rather tha
thought, and what progress there was in the world of ideas wa
restricted mainly to the theme of political theory. With th
return of the traditional order the streams of pure scholarship
dammed up in the years of war and stress, resumed their flov
with added impetus.

The gap between the two periods separated by war were bridged by the titanic figure of Thomas Hobbes. This formidable scholar and controversialist was born in the year of the Spanish Armada, and in his youth worked with Bacon, translating some of the famous essays into Latin; but he lived to be a nonagenarian, dying in 1679.

Hobbes was first and foremost a classical scholar. His knowledge of Latin and Greek was profound; several of his books were written in Latin, and during his long lifetime he translated both Homer and Thucydides. But early in his career he turned to mathematics, and thence to the natural sciences. He travelled widely on the Continent; in Italy he met Galileo, and in France he corresponded with Descartes. From the beginning of the English troubles onwards he produced his works of philosophy, in both Latin and English, discussing the nature of man, of matter and of society.

It was, however, in the realm of political philosophy that Hobbes made his greatest impact. When civil war threatened he discreetly withdrew himself from his native country, taking refuge in Paris. He was a convinced Royalist but not the sort of man to brave death for his beliefs. He preferred to observe the course of events from a safe distance, and in contemplating the anarchy of rebellion followed by the success of Cromwell's dictatorship he allowed his views to mature; from a monarchist he developed into an authoritarian. In 1651 he published his most famous work, *Leviathan*, in which, armed with the force of his training and philosophy, he argued the case for absolute monarchy as cogently as it has ever been presented. The life of man in his natural state, he averred in a celebrated passage, was 'solitary, poor, nasty, brutish, and short'. Only strong and unfettered authority could keep him from anarchy; to impose order, the sovereign in any society must be sole legislator, ruler and judge.

Leviathan made an enormous impression, which was reinforced by the superb prose in which it was written. Hobbes was one of the finest masters of English of his time, writing in the new style which was to be perfected by Dryden: always th right word in the right place, with balanced sentences free fro unnecessary embellishment.

It was, however, neither the brilliance of his writing nor th extreme nature of his political views that aroused so muc controversy and made the author of *Leviathan* so suspect in th minds of scholars of Restoration England. What brought hi enemies, with whom he was always ready to do battle, was th suspicion, amounting almost to conviction, that he was a atheist. This charge he vehemently denied; but certainly h views were unorthodox. It was part of the theme of *Leviatha* that religion, like everything else, must be wholly subordinat to the paramount civil authority; spiritual power could not b independent of the temporal. This hardly constituted atheism and it was after all a central point in Anglicanism that th sovereign was Supreme Governor of the Church. Nevertheles such opinions went too far for contemporary philosophers, wh could stomach almost any speculation except doubt of the trut of Christianity. Hobbes was suspected of more than doubt.

A more attractive figure, next to Hobbes in intellectua reputation and in many ways his superior, was Robert Boyle An Anglo-Irish aristocrat, Boyle was a younger son of the firs Earl of Cork, one of the most influential magnates in Ireland His main concern was pure science; he had little interest i politics or the public affairs of the day. He has been called 'th founder of modern chemistry', and in the early years of th Restoration he produced his monumental book *The Usefulness o Experimental Natural Philosophy*. This was followed by hi *History of Cold, The Sceptical Chymist, Experiments on Colour* and many more technical works.

At the same time his interests were not limited to his chose subject. He too was an all-round scholar, a Latinist and connoisseur of the arts. Unlike Hobbes he was a fervent Chris tian, and he took a particular interest in missionary activities al over the world, helping to promote the translation of the Bibl not only into Arabic but into various little-known languages o

R. CHR: WREN.
SURVEYOR GENERAL of
Royal Buildings .
ed the 22.ºof Feb.ʸ 1722. aged 91.

Sir Christopher Wren, painted by G. Kneller. At the time of the
Restoration, Wren, a mathematician and astronomer, had as yet given
little thought to architecture.

Engraving of the Sheldonian Theatre, Oxford, by D. Loggan. Wren's

the Orient, including even Malay. While his travels were mainly in Europe, he seems to have been specially attracted to the East. He was at one time a director of the East India Company.

Boyle, a modest and retiring scholar, was attacked for his religious views, which inclined towards Calvinism; but as a man he was universally popular. John Evelyn wrote of him that 'all was tranquil, easy, serious, discreet and profitable; so as besides Mr. Hobbes, whose hand was against everybody, and admired nothing but his own, . . . I do not remember he had the least antagonist'.

The advance in scientific scholarship was epitomized at the time of the Restoration in the foundation of the Royal Society for Promoting Natural Knowledge, generally known from then until the present day as 'the Royal Society', of which Boyle was one of the earliest fellows. Controversy has raged over the ancestry of the Royal Society, but it is now generally accepted that its origins lay in Oxford and that its spiritual father was Francis Bacon. In the 1650s, while England at large was in the throes of political transition, a group of Oxford scholars devoted themselves to the study of Bacon's ideas under the leadership of John Wilkins, Warden of Wadham College. When the Restoration came they formed themselves into an organized body in London, and in 1662 this body was granted a charter by Charles II, himself keenly interested in the natural sciences.

The study and development of Baconian philosophy in its widest aspects was the prime objective of the Royal Society: no less than the interpretation of all natural phenomena in the light of human reason. All science was thus its province; and in this, as it claimed, it was a true innovator. In his address to the King on the occasion of the presentation of the charter, Lord Brouncker, the first president, declared: 'This Society is already taken notice of and famous throughout all the learned parts of Europe: the first foundation of the greatest improvement of learning and arts that they are capable of, and which hath never heretofore been attempted by any.'

5

The Royal Society lived up to its name and its charter; it enjoyed genuine royal patronage. It was not only King Charles who took a personal interest in its proceedings. His cousin Prince Rupert was a practising scientist; he was elected a fellow in 1665, and many of his inventions and experiments were discussed by the Society.

Most of the leading intellectuals of the day were fellows or members of the Royal Society. They included, in addition to Boyle, Christopher Wren, John Evelyn, John Dryden, Edmund Waller, Sir Kenelm Digby, John Locke, Sir Robert Moray, Robert Hooke and Samuel Pepys; Isaac Newton, still in his teens at the time of the Restoration, became a fellow a little later. The first secretary was Dr Wilkins.

One eminent scholar who stood aloof was Hobbes. As usual he preferred to plough a lone furrow. Moreover he despised and attacked the whole range of university teaching, and in doing so earned the enmity of the academic world in general. He had no use for the Royal Society, and the Royal Society had no use for him.

The Society held its weekly meetings at Gresham College in the City of London, and here every contemporary philosophical and scientific problem was discussed. Bacon had laid great stress on the value of experiment, and experiments by the score were carried out at Gresham College. Some of the earliest ones invited ridicule. In one case a spider was placed within a circle of unicorn's horn (how this horn was procured is not recorded) to see if it could walk out; contrary to the traditional belief, it did. But this was the age of innumerable such superstitions and folk tales; of belief in witchcraft, necromancy and alchemy. Part of the Royal Society's task was to test such beliefs and find out if there was any basis for them.

On one occasion at least the King himself indulged in some raillery. Pepys records that: 'Gresham College he mightily laughed at for spending time only in weighing ayre, and doing nothing else since they sat.' It was a typical piece of royal badinage, but the weighing of air was by no means a pointless experiment; the investigation of atmospheric pressure was the beginning of the development of the use of steam.

Sir Christopher Wren, perhaps the most distinguished of early Fellows of the Royal Society, lives in history as probably the greatest of all British architects; but at the time of the Restoration he had given little thought to architecture. His reputation then was concerned mostly with mathematics but also with astronomy. Two years younger than Charles II, he was twenty-eight when the King came back into his realm, and he was perhaps the most brilliant of all the young men then taking their place in the intellectual life of London.

He started with advantages. His father was Dean of Windsor and his uncle, Matthew Wren, Bishop of Ely; both suffered deprivation under the Puritans, but young Christopher thus had the entrée to the highest Anglican circles, which stood him well when the Church of England came back into its own. Meanwhile, unconcerned with politics, he himself suffered little from the troubles of the times. After leaving Westminster, where he was one of Busby's pupils, he devoted himself to the study of his chosen subjects, but in addition to arithmetic, geometry and astronomy he proved himself a competent classical scholar; he also mastered the elements of engineering, and under the tuition of Charles Scarburgh he interested himself in medical science. Scarburgh had been a pupil of William Harvey, discoverer of the circulation of the blood, the most illustrious physician of the century, who died three years before the Restoration.

Thus when Wren went up to Oxford in 1649 he was already known for his well-stocked mind and his intellectual versatility. 'That prodigious young Scholar', was how John Evelyn described him in the early 1650s. His college was Wadham, and there he came under the influence of the Warden, John Wilkins, soon becoming a shining light in the circle of philosophers and scientists who at the Restoration developed into the Royal Society. In 1657, at the age of twenty-five, he was appointed Professor of Astronomy at Gresham College; a post which four years later he exchanged for a similar professorship at Oxford. He was thus in residence at Gresham when the newly formed Royal Society took up its abode there, and of that organization he became, almost automatically, a founder member.

During these years he indulged in inventions and experiments of a practical kind and of remarkable variety. He produced meteorological instruments for measuring rainfall; he devised improvements to the telescope; he conducted new experiments in the art of etching; he invented a 'weather-clock'. It was hardly surprising that the Royal Society regarded him as its most eminent fellow.

Wren's entrance into his most famous sphere of action arose out of his geometrical studies. This was fully in accordance with the ideas of his time. Inigo Jones, the greatest British architect of the first half of the seventeenth century, had been from the first an artist rather than a scientist or mathematician; but Jones was exceptional. To the seventeenth-century mind architecture was a branch of mechanics, of geometrical calculation; a matter of working out rules and applying them to the design of buildings.

So it was that, at a time when his reputation lay entirely in other fields, Wren was offered official work of an architectural nature. King Charles's marriage to the Portuguese Princess Catherine brought the port of Tangier into English possession, and the young mathematician was suggested for the important task of surveying the harbour and designing new fortifications. This offer he declined, perhaps because at this moment of his career he did not want to leave Oxford; but it was soon succeeded by another nearer home. Gilbert Sheldon, Bishop of London and the most influential prelate in the Church of England, wished to make a memorable gift to his old university, and Christopher Wren was invited to design what became known as the Sheldonian Theatre.

This building, which stands today as the earliest of Wren's architectural work, was intended as the setting for formal university functions, and Wren decided to build it on the lines of a Roman theatre. Such theatres, however, were open to the sky; Wren showed his originality and his geometrical ingenuity in providing a roof of his own invention to harmonize with the general plan of a classical building. The result was acclaimed as a masterpiece. Evelyn, a lifelong friend and admirer of Wren, described it some years later as 'a fabric comparable to any of this kind of former ages, and doubtless exceeding any of the present'.

Wren showed his model of the Sheldonian to the Royal Society in 1663; during the next three years he designed a number of buildings in Oxford and Cambridge, and in 1665 he paid a visit to Paris. This appears to have been his only journey abroad; he was not one of the travelled scientists of the Restoration period. But in Paris he met and talked with Bernini, the most famous architect of his time, who was in the French capital at the invitation of Louis XIV to design the rebuilding of part of the Louvre. This meeting had a considerable influence on his ideas.

These were the beginnings of the architectural career of one of Britain's greatest artists. By the time the disaster of the Fire of London presented him with his pre-eminent opportunity, he was accepted as the country's leading designer of buildings and the man most fitted to preside over the rebirth of the city. His tremendous achievements during the rest of his lifetime—he lived as long as Hobbes and died in the reign of George I— belong to a later period of history. Success never marred his character. In old age as in youth he was modest and unassuming, of a genial and friendly nature; he never bothered himself with public affairs, and his life was singularly free from controversy and acrimony.

Sir Christopher Wren so dominated the architectural scene in the reign of Charles II that his contemporaries have been almost forgotten. There were, however, other eminent architects in his time, many of whom had made their mark long before he turned to the art for which he is now remembered.

The names of John Webb, Hugh May and Sir Roger Pratt have fallen into not-altogether-deserved obscurity.

The chief figure in the world of architecture in the seventeenth century was the Surveyor or Surveyor-General. In earlier times this post was equivalent to that of master-mason or master-carpenter; little distinction was made between the design of buildings and their erection. Inigo Jones, however, as Charles I's Surveyor had brought a new dimension to the work, and architecture had acquired the professional dignity to which it was entitled, though it was still approached from the mathematical and engineering viewpoint rather than the artistic.

There had been little important building in the stern days of war and Republicanism, and after Jones's death the Surveyorship, in the hands of a negligible practitioner named Embree, had fallen into disrepute. With the Restoration an age of new grandeur dawned. The royal residences were all in need of repair, while the grandees who rose to eminence under the restored regime were ready and anxious to establish stately homes for themselves and their descendants. Obviously the Surveyor-General would once more become a personage of importance, the man in charge of the Office of Works and the arbiter of architectural taste. The post was given, surprisingly, to Sir John Denham, a competent poet but without achievement or distinction in the profession of which he was now the official head. It was said that the King had obligations to him, incurred during the years of exile, and felt compelled to provide him with a lucrative position. In the event Denham produced only one building of note, Burlington House in Piccadilly; and how far the design was really his is a matter of doubt.

The man who should have been appointed Surveyor, certainly in his own view but also in that of most good judges, was John Webb, the most experienced English architect living. Webb had for a quarter of a century been the pupil and assistant of Jones, and throughout this period had been closely associated with the work of the master. After Jones's death he had designed a number of important houses on his own account, including

Lamport Hall for Sir Justinian Isham and Belvoir for the Earl of Rutland. After the Restoration his most important work was the King Charles Building at Greenwich. He was nearly fifty when the King returned to England, and though disappointed of the post he deserved, he continued to work as assistant to Denham. In the words of a recent authority on British architecture, Sir John Summerson, 'from the point of view of technique and scholarship he was head and shoulders above all other designers practising at the date of the Restoration.'

Hugh May became Paymaster under Sir John Denham in 1660. Like his superior he was inexperienced in designing, but unlike him he soon became one of the finest architects of the age. In the days before the Fire he was still learning his craft, but in 1663 he built for the vintner Sir John Shaw one of the best country houses of the period, Eltham Lodge in Kent. This was followed by Berkeley House in Piccadilly.

May was an elegant figure in society, cousin of the courtier Baptist May; the greater part of his architectural work was for private patrons. Later in the reign of Charles II, however, he was the central figure in the extensive rebuilding carried out at Windsor Castle under the King and Prince Rupert.

Another architect who moved in high social circles was Sir Roger Pratt, a close friend of John Evelyn and a cousin of Sir George Pratt of Coleshill in Berkshire. He was much more a student of the theory of architecture than was May or (in his earlier days) Wren. When the Great Civil War broke out he found it prudent to leave England, and until 1649 he travelled on the Continent, where with admirable thoroughness he studied the new ideas for building which were being developed in France and Italy.

Meanwhile Coleshill, Sir George Pratt's country house, was destroyed by fire. Sir George immediately embarked on rebuilding, and Inigo Jones was called in to advise on design. This, however, was at the very end of Jones's life, and it is now acknowledged that this palatial mansion was substantially the work of Roger Pratt, who returned to England at this time full of the knowledge which he had accumulated in Europe and which he now put at the disposal of his cousin. The house was completed in 1662.

Pratt built a few more country houses, and in 1664 took on his most ambitious project, the great mansion planned by King Charles's first Lord Chancellor in his days of glory. Clarendon House, dominating Piccadilly, was the most imposing private dwelling in London. It was completed in 1667, only just before the great statesman fell from grace. Sixteen years later it was demolished.

Shortly afterwards Pratt, honoured by the King with a knighthood, designed a house for himself and retired into private life. His importance lies in the new ideas he introduced and the notebooks he left on the science of architecture.

From the work of these architects there evolved a style that was distinctively English, though ironically enough the prime influence arose from foreign ideas. The Restoration period was unquestionably a great era for architecture in the country, even though its finest fruits were to blossom in later years. The seventeenth century saw the awakening of a new spirit in the design of buildings. Before that time the influence of Gothic, the style in which the great cathedrals of the Middle Ages had been built, had reigned supreme. But this sublime tradition had outlived its strength; it had degenerated into the debased imitation known as 'Tudor Gothic'. New ideas were urgently needed. They were found in the century of the Stewarts, first and foremost under the leadership of Inigo Jones.

Jones had travelled in Italy, and he introduced into England a type of architecture founded on the work of the sixteenth-century Italian Palladio, who had laid down rules of design. Instead of the straight lines and pointed arches of the Gothic, buildings took on a more rounded outline, with graceful pillars and regular façades. The domination of what became known as Palladianism was a later development in English architecture, but its foundations were laid by Jones.

When the Restoration came, and fresh incentives to building

were found in the enthusiasm inspired by the opening of a more splendid era, the ambitions of newly-enriched noblemen, the expansion of Oxford and Cambridge colleges and the need for bigger and more beautiful churches, foreign influences were again in evidence. The men who stood out as the new architects had in many cases shared the exile of the King and seen the work being done abroad, and the court of Louis XIV was a shining example of magnificence. Wren was an original genius whose achievements cannot be fitted into any exact category, but even his methods were to some extent influenced by his one visit to Paris and his contact with Bernini.

French influence on Restoration architecture was the greatest, but there was also Italian and Dutch, together with the semi-Italian legacy left by Inigo Jones. French and Italian examples were paramount in the ideas of Pratt; Dutch in those of May, whose style has been characterized as Dutch Palladianism. In domestic architecture the new men worked in brick and stone; half-timbered building, which had hitherto prevailed, fell into disuse.

Between them Webb, May, Pratt, Wren and their contemporaries produced work that embodied the best elements of what was being done in Europe. Yet at the same time it was sharply distinguished from the prevailing tendencies abroad. The seventeenth century on the Continent was the age of Baroque. It is not an easy word to define. Sir George Clark, general editor of the *Oxford History of England*, did so as lucidly as anybody when he said that Baroque 'is best described not as a style, but as a tendency which may express itself in any style and which has overtaken most styles in their later stages. It is the tendency to extravagance and exuberance, to sweeping curves and swelling surfaces, loaded with ornament and ignoring or concealing the limitations of structure.' From this tendency to extravagance and exuberance English architecture remained singularly free. 'English Baroque', if there ever was such a thing, was always restrained by that sense of economy and practicability which is usually considered a national characteristic. Thus was produced a school of architecture which had no counterpart in any other country.

England owes a great deal to those architects of the Restoration period who struck out on their own, dignified the country-side, constructed great buildings of distinction and originality in the towns and cities, and enabled their successors to develop and continue a truly English tradition. The same, unfortunately, cannot be said of the pictorial arts. The seventeenth century, whatever else it may have been, was not a great age of English painting. There was indeed a school of court portraiture, though English artists had little enough to do with it; and the appearance of the splendid buildings that were going up was preserved in their original setting by some noble pictures. But there was little or no landscape painting in the general sense, and no school of genre-painting. The artists who in France and Holland portrayed the ordinary life of their contemporaries in town and country for the benefit of posterity found no echo in England, at least so far as painters of major talent were concerned.

With one shining exception, and that in what must be called a minor and constricted field, the leading painters of Restoration England were foreign. The tradition went back to an earlier period. Charles I, the pre-eminent royal connoisseur of his time, had filled his galleries with masterpieces from all over Europe, and had invited the finest European artists to his court. Two of these, both Flemish, stood out above the rest. Peter Paul Rubens, amid the multifarious activities of his busy life, had contributed his superb canvases in honour of the English King's father to the ceiling of the new Banqueting House in Whitehall. Sir Anthony Van Dyck had settled down in London as court painter to King Charles and during the ten years before the Civil War had produced a series of portraits unrivalled in English history.

Van Dyck's successor as court painter at Whitehall was Peter Lely, who in spite of the name by which he is known came also from Flanders. His family was that of van der Faes; 'Lely', which he adopted on coming to England, was the name of a house owned by the family.

When the Restoration came Lely, whose assumed name was often written as 'Lilly', had been in England for many years. He arrived either during the war years or soon afterwards, and about 1650 acquired a house in Covent Garden which he occupied till his death in London thirty years later. He worked for a number of wealthy patrons, the most important of whom was the Earl of Northumberland. During this period he painted portraits of many of the leading figures of the day, including Oliver Cromwell.

The change of regime made no difference to Lely, who had not interested himself in English politics. In 1661 he was granted a pension of £200 a year as official portrait painter to Charles II, who knighted him later in his reign. In the years that followed the Restoration there was hardly a major dignitary of Whitehall who did not sit to Lely, and he also painted nearly all the ladies of the court. The features of the royal mistresses are largely known from the work of this fashionable society portraitist; though incompletely, for his integrity as an artist is suspect. Van Dyck had been a flatterer in his work, and so probably was Lely. Excellent artist though he was, there is a sameness about his female portraits that has drawn some harsh words from critics of later ages. When Pepys saw his series of portraits of the maids of honour, commissioned by the Duchess of York, he summed them up in four words: 'good, but not like.' Among Lely's female sitters those who showed most vitality were those who were willing or anxious to be painted wearing few clothes or none. His nude portrait, believed to be of Nell Gwyn or Barbara Palmer, is famous.

When the Second Dutch War broke out Lely was given, by the Duke of York, a commission of which he made better use. This was a series of portraits of the senior officers—Prince Rupert, Lord Sandwich, Sir William Penn and others—who had shone in the Battle of Lowestoft. These drew higher praise from Pepys. 'Sir W. Batten and Sir Tho. Allen and I to Mr

Lillys the painter's,' he wrote on 18 April 1666, 'and there saw the heads, some finished and all begun, of the Flaggmen in the late great fight with the Duke of Yorke against the Dutch. The Duke of York hath them done to hang in his chamber, and very finely they are done indeed.' They are probably Lely's finest portraits.

Lely's portrayals of the leading figures of his day are important historical documents, but he was perhaps spoilt by success. In his young days on the continent he had been a landscape painter of charm and freshness, but this style he abandoned for more lucrative work. A close friend of Hugh May, he figured in the world of fashion and made a comfortable income. At the same time he undoubtedly dominated the art world of his day.

Other contemporary painters were mostly of little importance. Lely maintained a studio in London, both at this period and later in his prosperous career, where he and his pupils, who were usually Dutch or Flemish, worked together. It is often hard to say where his own painting ends and theirs begins; and as time went on, and commissions came in greater profusion, he probably handed more and more work over to them. He would paint the face, and perhaps the hands, and depute the rest to his staff. Such was the nature of court portraiture.

There were, however, a few English painters of some note who were working at this time. One was John Greenhill, who specialized in theatrical portraits. Others were Isaac Fuller, few of whose paintings survive, and John Hales, who was patronized by Pepys and painted his wife. Michael Wright, a Scottish Catholic and a cosmopolitan, painted members of leading Catholic families such as the Arundells of Wardour; his work was above the average, but the devotional nature of some of his pictures counted against him in Protestant England. A woman painter of moderate talent was Mary Beale, whose husband, a Government servant, was a scholar and connoisseur of art.

Such landscape painters as there were came from abroad.

One of the most notable was the Dutchman Hendrick Danckerts, who painted many pictures of Hampton Court, Windsor and Greenwich for King Charles II.

A more important artist, but one more memorable in the field of engraving than of painting, was Wenceslaus Hollar. He came from Bohemia, having been born in Prague in 1607. His youth was spent in various parts of Europe, and in 1636 he entered the service of the Earl of Arundel when that most cultivated of travellers and art-collectors was on a diplomatic mission to Vienna. From then on Hollar was from time to time a visitor to England, and by 1660 he had become a permanent resident.

Hollar's output was immense, and his etchings are more important as historical documents than, perhaps, the work of any other artist of the day. They are mostly small in compass; Aubrey, who knew him personally, records that 'he was very short-sighted, and did work so curiously that the curiosity of his work is not to be judged without a magnifying-glass'. He was a consummate draughtsman, who recorded the details of buildings, of scenes of town and country, and of public events with minute accuracy. His pictures of London life and of the countryside, in water-colours as well as drawings and etchings, are of an interest to the historian transcending even his talent as an artist. As a topographer he excelled all his contemporaries, and the many maps he drew of London and other towns are of the utmost value.

No other artist of his kind approached Hollar in talent; etching in England did not reach its apogee till a later age. However a new form of etching did appear in the country at this time. This was mezzotint, introduced to England by Prince Rupert and probably invented by him, which John Evelyn heralded in his book *Sculptura*, published in 1662. The new method did not produce much art of value at this time, though Prince Rupert himself was responsible for some good examples. Its full development came in the eighteenth century.

Sculpture in the Restoration period was largely influenced by

Bernini; and in this field yet again the principal artists were foreign. Typical of them was Caius Gabriel Cibber, the father of the actor and dramatist Colley Cibber, who came to England from Denmark. There were, however, some native artists at work; chief among them was John Bushnell, who had studied in Italy during the interregnum. Much of the sculpture achieved at this time was in the form of tomb effigies, most of which were anonymous. After the Fire of London, however, a new opportunity was provided for sculptors, including Bushnell and Cibber, who were employed in creating statues of monarchs and other notables to adorn the new buildings in the city.

It was left to the school of miniature painters, and pre-eminently to one practitioner, to uphold the honour of English pictorial art. The miniature, in the form of water-colour painted on vellum, had from early Tudor times been an English speciality. Developing out of the exquisite manuscript illuminations of the Middle Ages, these tiny portraits came to be used as love tokens and as court gifts to foreign rulers or diplomats. In the Elizabethan-Jacobean era the art rose to new heights in the work of Nicholas Hilliard.

With the coming of the Caroline age more sophisticated techniques developed, with the use of more varied pigments and the development of new methods of colouring. In this intermediate period the principal name is that of John Hoskins, the details of whose life are shadowy but who painted many miniatures of sovereigns, courtiers and rulers in the reign of Charles I and under the Cromwellian regime. He was influenced by Van Dyck, and made copies of the master's portraits in miniature form, including more than one of Queen Henrietta Maria. In his case attribution in particularly difficult because he had a son with the same Christian name whose style was virtually indistinguishable from his own.

John Hoskins the elder, who was born probably in the last years of the sixteenth century, lived into the Restoration era, dying in 1665; so far as is known he went on painting miniatures to the end. His fame, however, rests not on his own achievements but on his introducing to the world of culture a far finer artist than himself.

Hoskins had two nephews of the name of Cooper, and the most painstaking research has revealed little of their early years. Nothing is known of their parentage or places of birth, or of the circumstances in which they entered the household of their uncle John Hoskins. All that has come to light is that from about the beginning of Charles I's reign they were living in Hoskins's house in London and that they produced their earliest works under his tuition.

Alexander Cooper, the elder of the two brothers, left England in his twenties and appears to have spent the rest of his life on the Continent. He had a high talent and served as a court painter successively in Holland, Sweden and Denmark. The few miniatures surviving which can be certainly ascribed to him compare favourably with those of other members of the family. He died in 1660.

His younger brother Samuel is the one painter of the reign of Charles II to whom the epithet 'great' can be indisputably assigned. His genius was fully recognized by his contemporaries, and the chorus of praise has echoed down to our own time. 'Limning' was the word usually employed to describe miniature painting at this time. Aubrey knew Samuel Cooper well, as he knew most of the more illustrious of his contemporaries. His 'brief life' of his 'honoured friend' is tantalizingly brief and tells us nothing; but there are numerous references to him in the other biographies, and hardly a single one which does not describe him as 'the prince of limners'. In his life of Hobbes Aubrey writes:

Amongst other of his acquaintance I must not forget our common friend Mr Samuel Cowper, the prince of limners of this last age, who drew his picture as like as art could afford, and one of the best pieces that ever he did: which his majesty, at his returne, bought of him, and conserves as one of his great rarities in his closet at Whitehall.

Samuel Cooper quickly matured into one of the leading artists of his day. He was born in 1609, and by the 1630s his reputation was established. About this time he appears to have travelled on the continent and studied the work of Bernini among others; he was already, as John Hoskin's pupil, under the influence of Van Dyck. In 1642 or thereabouts he left his uncle's house and set up for himself in Covent Garden. According to one authority Hoskins became jealous of his obvious superiority and dissolved the partnership they had formed. Be this as it may, Cooper thenceforward took an independent line, and till his death thirty years later turned out an uninterrupted series of incomparable miniature portraits. Like other artists of his time he allowed political changes to flow over his head without disturbing his output. His portraits of Cromwell were considered the best that were done in any medium of the Protector, and when the King returned he was at the height of his fame. A few years later he was established at court as 'His Majesty's Lymner'.

By general consent Cooper stands at the head of all painters who have worked in miniature. His portraits of King Charles II and the various members of his court, male and female, excel those of Lely as much as they do the work of his great predecessor in his own medium, Hilliard. He prepared his own materials, made his own brushes (or 'pencils'), and used an ivory palette; and in doing so brought the technique of miniature painting to a degree that was never improved upon. His portraits have a delicacy, an understanding of character, a perfection of colouring, and a grandeur of design that no other miniature painter ever achieved.

Cooper's achievements were not limited to his chosen form of art. A few drawings survive; they are mostly portraits of members of the Hoskins family and show the same quality of delineating character as do the miniatures. He also drew King Charles's head for the coinage, on which occasion Evelyn recorded that he himself was in Cooper's studio and 'had the honour to hold the candle while it was doing, [Cooper] choosing to do this at night and by candle light, for the better finding out the shadows'.

Music too came within the sphere of his interests. It was said that he was 'reckoned one of the best lutenists of his time'. He was a man of wide culture, a glittering figure in the glittering intellectual circles of the day. Yet his personality remains elusive. Everybody respected him; it would seem that everybody who knew him liked him. Yet anecdotes that might reveal the man himself are lacking.

The finest miniature painter after Cooper was Thomas Flatman, some of whose portraits were confused with those of the master. Flatman like Cooper was a man of versatile culture; a satirist and poet of distinction; a Fellow of the Royal Society; a gifted amateur in many fields; of melancholy temperament and deep religious faith. Others at this time were Richard Gibson, a dwarf less than four feet in height, whose daughter Susan (of normal size) followed him as a miniaturist at a later date; Cornelius Johnson, English by birth but of Dutch descent, whose career was finishing at the time of the Restoration; and David Des Granges from Guernsey.

Their work redeemed the general lack of pictorial talent that characterized the era. And Samuel Cooper shines in solitary splendour as the greatest artist of his day.

There remains music. By no criterion can the era be called a great age for English music. It could boast no composer of real eminence; the most distinguished in the seventeenth century, Henry Purcell, was one year old at the Restoration. Yet music played as large a part in the lives of the English people as it has ever done. 'Of this beauty,' Sir Arthur Bryant has written, speaking of the colourful nature of the Restoration scene, 'music was queen.' One has only to glance through the diary of Pepys, admittedly a music-lover, to see how song and dance, and the playing of various instruments, pervaded the life of his day. On the village green the pipe and tabor were constantly heard. At court and in the houses of the nobility the gentry sang to the lute and the spinet. Trained choirs came back into their own in cathedrals and churches. The great age of the madrigal had been that of Elizabeth and James, but the airs of Wilbye and Dowland were still sung up and down the country. One of Charles II's first acts was to establish a string orchestra of twenty-four players in imitation of the *vingt-quatre violons du roi* whom he had heard and admired when he was the guest of Louis XIV.

The violin, which had been the particular instrument of the aristocracy in the earlier years of the century, was now coming into more general use. Apart from this and the spinet and the ubiquitous lute, there was a rich profusion of instruments available. The virginals were akin to the harpsichord, the word being applied to any keyboard instrument in which the strings were plucked by plectra. The viol, as distinct from the violin, enjoyed great popularity. Wind instruments included the cornet, the flute, the flageolet and the sackbut.

Church music flourished. It had never been altogether suppressed—under Puritan rule Anglican ritual had been interrupted, cathedral choirs disbanded, and in many cases organs destroyed; but this had depended very largely on the strength of local feeling. Music itself was not a target of Puritan fanaticism. Cromwell was devoted to it, and so were many of his leading followers. Where it could be reconciled with religious susceptibilities it was left unmolested. At York and Lincoln Cathedrals, and even at St Paul's in London, the organs were allowed to remain, although suspended from use. The arch-Puritan William Prynne, to whom masques and plays were the work of the devil, conceded in his *Histriomastix*: 'That Musicke of itselfe is lawful, usefull, and commendable, no man, no Christian dares denie, since the Scriptures, Fathers, and generally all Christian, all Pagan authors extant, do with one consent averre it.'

Ecclesiastical music, therefore, was rather developed than restored. Choirs gave tongue in praise of the restoration of Anglican worship; organs were brought back into use, and a golden age of organ-building dawned. The Presbyterians stood aloof. According to Anthony à Wood the Oxford antiquary, 'they compared the organ to the whining of pigs; their singing to that of a jovial crew in a blind ale-house.' But by the generality of a song-loving nation the harmony of church ritual was greeted with joyful thanksgiving.

Secular music, of a higher kind than that of the village green, took on a new lease of life. Here as in other aspects of artistic culture the prime influence came from the continent. The King and his courtiers had tasted the delights that good music could give during their years of exile, and soon after the Restoration public concerts where the best of European music could be heard began to be given in London. They started modestly with meetings held in a house near St Paul's Cathedral, and from there they rapidly spread.

Opera likewise made its appearance. It had its predecessor, so far as England was concerned, in the masques of which the first two Stewart kings had been so fond; but performances of French and Italian opera were a different thing. These did not become a regular part of London life till later in the century; but the first tentative advances were made during the reign of Charles II.

The composers of this age did not make much mark; but there were men of talent among them. Henry Cooke, who was appointed Master of the Children of the Chapel Royal at the Restoration, was the leading music teacher of the time. His pupil Pelham Humfrey, who succeeded him in the post, was sent by Charles II to study music in France and Italy. Humfrey died in 1674 at the age of twenty-seven, but he left behind him a large quantity of anthems and secular music. John Blow, who succeeded him at the Chapel Royal, was the principal teacher of Henry Purcell.

An amateur composer of note was Robert Creyghton, Professor of Greek at Cambridge, who composed services and anthems. John Eccles wrote incidental pieces for the theatre and, as Master of the King's Band, set official odes to music.

English music has seldom played a leading part in European

culture. But the age of Purcell and that which followed it, when the long residence of Handel in England gave it a cosmopolitan flavour, raised it to perhaps its highest point. And the foundations were laid at the time of the Restoration.

Public Order
and National Defence

Which is the basest Creature, Man, or Beast?
Birds feed on Birds, Beasts on each other prey;
But savage Man alone, does Man betray . . .
For Hunger, or for Love They bite or tear,
Whilst wretched Man is still in Arms for Fear:
For Fear he arms, and is of Arms afraid;
From Fear, to Fear, successively betray'd.

John Wilmot, Earl of Rochester

In the autumn of 1660 the atmosphere of the area around
Charing Cross was becoming increasingly polluted. The residents of the neighbouring streets were used to the normal
London smells, but the continual reek of burning flesh and
bowels was becoming a little too much for them; so they put
in a petition asking that the proceedings which had been causing
the trouble should be continued elsewhere. The kindly government acceded to the request, and for the remainder of its run
the show was transferred to the more customary Tyburn.

The spectacle, which the citizens of Westminster had greatly
enjoyed until it became unpleasant to their nostrils, was the
execution of the regicides guilty of the murder of Charles I.
The court had decreed that the criminals should suffer within
sight of the spot where their victim had been deprived of his
head. Eight men met their fate at Charing Cross before the
protest was made, and two more were hanged at Tyburn
before the King intervened.

Punishments were harsh in the reign of Charles II, and high
treason was considered the worst crime that could be committed.

A convicted traitor was addressed in the following words by the presiding judge:

> The judgement of this court is, and the court doth award, that you be led to the place from whence you came, and from thence to be drawn upon an hurdle to the place of execution; and there you shall be hanged by the neck, and being alive shall be cut down, and your privy members to be cut off, your entrails to be taken out of your body, and, you living, the same to be burned before your eyes, and your head to be cut off, your body to be divided into four quarters, and head and quarters to be disposed of at the pleasure of the King's Majesty, and the Lord have mercy upon your soul.

For women traitors the penalty was different. This was partly because the task of castrating a woman was beyond the capacity of even a seventeenth-century executioner; but the question of modesty was also taken into consideration. It was officially stated that 'the decency due to the sex forbids the exposing and publicly mangling their bodies'. So a convicted traitress was simply burned alive. How far this concession was appreciated is open to doubt.

As to the disposal of the heads and quarters of executed traitors 'at the pleasure of the King's Majesty', it was usual to display them at various conspicuous vantage spots. London Bridge was famous for its array of heads; the legs and arms might be set up on poles at Westminster Hall or at the City gates. Other cities and towns had their own customary show-places, though by 1660 it was exceptional for executions for treason to take place anywhere but in London.

Such sights as these were always liable to greet the law-abiding citizen when he walked abroad, and were calculated to instil in him a healthy respect for the authority of the state. And this, of course, was not all. High treason was rare, but lesser offences were everyday occurrences; and hanging was the penalty for a whole range of misdemeanours from murder

to shop-lifting. Such executions did not involve disembowel-
ment or mutilation. The victim was simply strung up and left
to die. The body might then be left for an indefinite period,
particularly if it was desired to impress the multitude with the
seriousness of the crime; but if there was no special reason for
leaving it, or if the gallows were wanted for somebody else,
it was cut down as soon as possible. Sometimes this was done
prematurely. Anthony à Wood tells of two very similar cases,
each involving the killing of an illegitimate baby. In the first:

> one Anne Green, a servant maid, was hang'd in the castle
> of Oxon, for murdering her bastard-child, begotten by
> Jeffry Reade grand-son to Sir Thomas Read of Duns-Tew in
> Oxfordshire. After she had suffer'd the law, she was cut
> downe, and carried away in order to be anatomiz'd by some
> young physitians, but they finding life in her, would not
> venter upon her, only so farr, as to recover her to life. Which
> being look'd upon as a great wonder, there was a relation
> of her recovery printed, and at the end several copies of
> verses made by the young poets of the Universitie were
> added.

The second girl, who 'was hang'd at Greenditch neare Oxon,
for murdering her infant-bastard', was not so lucky:

> . . . After shee was cut downe and taken away to be
> anatomiz'd, William Coniers a physitian of S. John's Coll
> and other young physitians, did in short time bring life into
> her. But the bayllives of the towne hearing of it, they went
> between 12 and one of the clock at night to the house where
> she laid, and putting her into a coffin carried her into Broken
> hayes, and by a halter about her neck drew her out of it, and
> hung her on a tree there. She then was so sensible of what
> they were about to do that she said, 'Lord, have mercy upon
> me,' etc. The women were exceedingly enraged at it, cut
> downe the tree wheron she was hang'd, and gave very

ill language to Henry Mallory one of the baillives when they saw him passing the streets, because he was the chief man that hang'd her. And because that he afterwards broke, or gave up his trade thro povertie (being a cutler), they did not stick to say that God's judgments followed him for the cruelty he shew'd to the poor maid.

The sight of rotting bodies, hanging on gallows at the various places of execution in London or the provinces, and throughout the countryside on wayside gibbets (where highwaymen were left dangling in chains till reduced to skeletons *pour encourager les autres*), was so familiar as to excite little comment.

Other spectacles, which the populace in general regarded with great glee, were the punishments for lesser crimes. Minor political offences, such as libelling public figures, were often punished by the pillory. The convicted person, who in serious cases might also have his ears cut off, had to stand for a given period against a pole crowned with a wooden board through holes in which his head and hands protruded; and the spectators were given a free hand to treat him as they wished. If he was popular he might be decked with nosegays; if he was not he was pelted with stones and less salubrious missiles. In the country, for petty misdemeanours, the stocks performed a similar function; while for vagrancy or for sexual lapses a man or woman might be whipped at the cart's tail 'until his or her body be bloody', as the law put it.

When it came to sexual offences, even animals were not immune if they infringed the moral code. Again to quote à Wood, who had an eye for the seamy side of life: 'in the beginning of this month a maid and a dog were hang'd at Tyburne for that the dog laid with her severall times.'

Imprisonment, for administrative reasons, was used less than in some other periods. In the conditions then prevailing it was simpler to fine a man, to flog him or to fetter him in the stocks or pillory, than to shut him up in limited accommodation and guard him. Prisons were, however, extensively employed to deal with political offenders and violators of the religious penal laws; the Quakers endured long spells of incarceration. Those committed for trial by local magistrates also had to be kept in custody pending the next assizes. Debtors and minor felons were sent to prison when there was no convenient alternative.

Prison conditions varied enormously, depending as they did very largely on the character of individual gaolers and local officials. Some of these were humane and enlightened, and did what they could to mitigate the miseries of the inmates. Discipline in most cases was not unduly rigorous; and if a man had money he could make himself almost as comfortable as he might be at home. His friends and family could visit him, and there was no limit to the amount and quality of food that could be brought to him provided he could pay for it. The gaolers themselves were usually ready to provide extra comforts for a consideration.

In some prisons, however, conditions were appalling. They were few and far between, and in times of turmoil they became revoltingly overcrowded. Prisoners were packed into cells regardless of space; in Bristol's Bridewell at one time fifty women shared four beds, those who could not squeeze in being compelled to lie in heaps on the filthy floor. Sanitation was primitive, and sometimes non-existent. Only the bare minimum of food was provided, and those who could not afford to get meals sent in lived near to starvation.

The penal system of Charles II's England represented one aspect of the history of a rough and virile people. The torture and brutality now seem almost incredible in their ferocity, particularly to a generation which has gone to the other extreme in leniency to the criminal. Yet there is a reverse side to the coin. Certain factors should always be taken into consideration.

In the first place it was not a question of savagery for savagery's sake. The brutal sentences, taken for granted over the centuries, had been devised in the dark ages when life had indeed been 'nasty, brutish and short' and violence was the natural order of things. That the more barbarous punishments had survived so long was the result of lack of imagination and the human conservatism of authority rather than any lust for cruelty. Laws do not disappear easily from the statute book.

Secondly, it is true to say that at this period, as at most if not all others, English justice was very much more humane than that to be found elsewhere. The fate of the evil-doer in this country, if he happened to be caught, was admittedly hard; but such atrocities as breaking on the wheel, common throughout Europe, or tearing a man to pieces by fastening his limbs to different horses which were then whipped into a stampede (as was done to the assassin of Henry IV of France), found no place in English law.

Thirdly, the infliction of frightening punishments constituted the only practical method of deterring the potential criminal and thus protecting the peace and security of the law-abiding citizen. Men and women are not naturally virtuous. If they are given the chance to commit crimes with impunity they will do so, as today is beginning to dawn even on the minds of politicians. And society's machinery for the prevention of crime has developed to a degree inconceivable in the seventeenth century.

England in that century could boast no police force. In the country the village constable, in the towns the bellman or watchman and the bailiff, had powers of arrest, as had magistrates and other local officials. But their efforts were usually futile; the organization, such as it was, could not be remotely compared with the establishment of a disciplined police force. The constable was in most cases a local tradesman, recruited (usually unwillingly) for unpaid community service for a limited period and with no training for his post; he was quite unfitted for the task of controlling his unruly neighbours. The night bellman of London was almost a music-hall joke. He pottered about the city with his lamp and his bell, calling the hours. Poets looked on him with affection. 'Along the dark and silent night,' were words put into his mouth by Herrick, 'With my lantern and my light, and the tinkling of my bell, Thus I walk and this I tell.' Milton wrote of 'the Belmans drousie charm, To bless the dores from nightly harm'. But if he was required to stray outside his primary duty, to take practical steps to bless the doors from nightly harm, he quickly made himself scarce. He was no match for the gangs of bully-boys that roamed the streets. Should he not get out of the way fast enough he was likely to find himself beaten with clubs, his lamp smashed and his head pushed into a ditch.

Bringing a criminal to justice was therefore no easy matter. But it could at least be ensured that if he was caught he would regret it. A potential wrongdoer might think twice if he knew that he ran the risk of being strangled to death at the end of a rope and perhaps having his eyes pecked out by birds of prey while he was dying, of being flogged into unconsciousness at the tail of a cart, of being pelted with stones and ordure while incapable of self-defence, of dying of suffocation or disease in an insanitary prison, perhaps of having his right hand cut off (the penalty for crimes committed in the presence of the King).

Such at least was the theory. How far it was true in practice must always be open to question. Measures to combat crime are liable to defeat their own object. The sight of decaying corpses swinging on gibbets may concentrate the mind of an intending robber wonderfully, and induce him to think again about his future plans; it may, on the other hand, become so familiar an experience that he ceases to think about it and regards the risk as all in the day's work. Brutal spectacles can undoubtedly brutalize the spectator. The state of lawlessness under King Charles II does not altogether inspire confidence in the methods of deterrence employed.

Unquestionably crime flourished in the Restoration period, though no more virulently than in most eras. In a great proportion of cases it involved violence. Life was cheap, and when theft itself was punished with death a thief could add murder to robbery without incurring any additional risk. Gangs, though not highly organized by modern standards, operated in town and country, and men of good will were compelled to carry swords at all times for protection against their assaults.

That there should be, in practice, one law for the rich and one for the poor was inevitable, given the conditions of the time. To some extent this was the case in theory too. Members of the House of Lords were tried by their peers, who in spite of political differences were inclined to be lenient to those of their own order. If a titled magnate committed high treason he seldom suffered the full penalty of the law; for the hanging and quartering was substituted, by the King's prerogative, the more dignified and less painful fate of death by the axe, even though the followers whom he had seduced from their allegiance might go through all the agonizing ritual.

It was, however, the mere nature of seventeenth-century society that created class distinctions in lawlessness. Great families held the predominant influence in the countryside, and if the heads of those families chose to step outside the law there was no power that could stop them. The more remote the district, the greater was the strength of the local magnate; and if he was of an anti-social disposition he might make his domain into a little kingdom and defy the central authorities with impunity. It was in this era that the Doones of Exmoor, immortalized by R. D. Blackmore, had their being. So far as the hard facts of history go, their deeds are almost unchronicled. Blackmore developed the theme of *Lorna Doone* from local folklore, amplified by his own powers of invention. Painstaking research, however, has revealed that the Doones, immigrants from Scotland, did exist, and did terrorize the Somerset countryside in very much the manner described. There is no reason to suppose that the novelist exaggerated.

In the country at large the most prominent criminal was the highwayman. On the lonely, unpoliced roads he had very much his own way, and the traveller took his life in his hands. If he had the wealth and position to do so he made his journeys attended by a retinue of armed retainers, but the more humble wayfarer, on horseback or riding in one of the coaches that were the normal mode of travel, was always liable to be set upon. Highwaymen had their intelligence services, which were sometimes extremely efficient. Roadside innkeepers were often their accomplices, and they had their doxies who worked as barmaids or chambermaids at the inns and could supply them with information. The approach of a coach was in most cases known well in advance.

Since their heyday highwaymen have figured as heroes of romance and this tradition started in their own time. The 'gentleman of the road' was not entirely an invention of later ages. Stories were told in the 1660s and onwards of their chivalry towards the ladies they robbed; they would treat them with courtesy, respect their honour, and escort them to safety after relieving them of their jewels. Claude Duval, a Frenchman who was hanged at Tyburn in 1670, was the classic example. His manners were perfect, and he was even said to have danced gracefully with one of his fair victims on Hounslow Heath. When he was finally caught, 'there was a great company of ladies, and these not of the meanest degree, that visited him in prison, interceded for his pardon, and accompanied him to the gallows.' But most of the stories about him were apocryphal.

There is no need to discredit all such tales; some of them certainly had foundation in fact. But one may doubt the dis-interestedness of highway courtesy. Those who are said to have practised it were practical professional men, and they acted accordingly. If time and opportunity offered, any woman who fell into a highwayman's hands, and was sufficiently personable, was probably raped without more ado; certainly this happened in a good many cases. But there was usually need to get away quickly after robbery was accomplished. In that case a little show of gallantry and kissing of hands would do no harm and might stand to the gentleman's credit when the day of reckoning came.

Stories of the polite behaviour of highwaymen arose at least in part from the undoubted fact that a great many of them were in fact gentlemen by birth. The problem of what to do with the younger sons always faced aristocratic houses. Families were large and cash resources not always adequate, and the English system ensured that the bulk of any fortune there was should go to the eldest. If his younger brother had not the talent to make a living at the bar, or sufficient cunning for a successful career in politics, he could find himself at a loose end. He might get a commission in the army or navy, but often there were just two alternatives—the church or the road. And the church was an overcrowded profession.

Most of the younger sons were gamblers, in the fashion of the time; and highway robbery held out at least a hope of recouping their losses at the gaming tables. A further factor that helped to make this form of crime an aristocratic profession was horsemanship. Members of noble families were brought up to be skilled riders, and could usually get possession of horses. Their inferiors, uneducated in equestrianism, were forced into less spectacular exploits. The humble footpad, who operated on the outskirts of towns, was the poor relation of the highwayman.

All this helps to explain the glamour attached to the calling of the knights of the road. In spite of the hardships they inflicted on harmless travellers, and the barbarities many of them committed, they inspired a regard that no other form of crime could boast. The Verney memoirs contain many references to kinsmen who had adopted the road as their means of livelihood, and highly reputable members of that distinguished family spoke of them with affection. Such was Fred Turville, a cousin, who was hanged in 1660. Another relative, Dick Hals, had a remarkably long run for his money before meeting the accustomed fate in 1685. When he died Sir Ralph Verney, the head of the family, wrote: 'I am sorry for Dick Hals, and wish he might have been transported. I trust God will forgive him, and keep us from such sad ends.' ''Tis pity such men should be hanged,' was the comment of the respectable John Verney on another execution of highwaymen.

These aristocratic criminals had their counterparts in the

towns. Here too they were able to get their way by means of
wealth and family influence, but they lacked the popularity of
the highwaymen; they could make themselves feared but not
loved. There was no romance attached to the London gangs
of bravos hired by an Earl of Rochester or a Duke of Buckingham to commit criminal assault on such respected figures as
John Dryden or the Duke of Ormonde. Such incidents were the
outcome of hate or vendetta, but sheer hooliganism accounted
for others. Young men of means and good family thought it
fun to wander, usually drunk, through the streets of London by
night, attack and perhaps rob late wayfarers, and beat or terrify
the bellmen. Buckingham was notorious for his escapades;
Buckhurst and Sedley were guilty on more than one occasion.

Disorderly behaviour, however, was not a monopoly of the
rich. The criminal classes of the Restoration were constantly
active. Thefts were frequent, and usually successful; burglaries,
robberies with violence, took place nightly. There were areas
of London where decent citizens dared not penetrate, where no
night bellman would dream of risking his life. The most
notorious was the district, stretching from the Temple to
Blackfriars, which became known as Alsatia. This was the
haunt of every kind of criminal. It was a sanctuary for debtors,
but it offered hospitality to anybody trying to escape the
consequences of his crimes. He was quite likely to be murdered
there by his fellow thugs, but at least the law could not touch
him.

The nature of Alsatia was partly dictated by the fact that it
had formerly been on the doorstep of the great Dominican
convent which gave its name to Blackfriars. The convent had
perished at the Reformation, but by then the hospitality of
the friars had resulted in the creation of a widespread slum
peopled by those profiting from the food and alms doled out
from the convent. There were other such areas whose inmates
had basked in the charity to which the older religious orders
were dedicated: one was the mass of narrow streets which
existed almost to within living memory behind Westminster

Abbey, where the Benedictine monks ministered for centuries to the poor.

A great deal of the metropolitan area's crime was concentrated across the river in Southwark. There stood the Marshalsea, most famous of prisons; in spite of which the borough had a reputation for greater laxity in the repression of crime than could be found in the City of London. Fugitives from justice thronged to the southern bank of the Thames.

Part of the attraction of Southwark lay in the row of brothels on Bankside. There were of course plenty of brothels north of the river; some of the highest-class houses were in Covent Garden. But the Bankside stews had a tradition of their own going back to the early Middle Ages. There had been, in fact, various attempts through the centuries to confine this trade to the one particular area; Bankside brothels were regulated by law, and it was thought desirable to congregate the ladies in one district where the ecclesiastical and secular authorities could keep an eye on them. Such attempts habitually failed, as did the move of Henry VIII in his last years to reverse the trend and clear Bankside of its age-old institutions. The ancient system continued virtually untramelled.

These brothels inevitably attracted the criminal element, and like the slum areas of London tended to become haunts of evil-doers. They were the scene of frequent riots, and many unpleasant characters found sanctuary in the hospitable arms of the lady inmates. This applied to the brothels of more northern houses also and might account for the periodical attacks made by the London apprentices (always obstreperous, and in their less puritanical moods ardent patrons of houses of pleasure) on houses that met with their disapproval. Or perhaps the grievances were merely concerned with overcharging or with health hazards. On one occasion a gang of these idle apprentices ran riot in Whetstone Park and wrecked every brothel they could find. When King Charles was told of the disorder he made the reasonable comment: 'Why do they go to them then?' And the matter was allowed to drop.

Treatment of the Poor: Whipping a Vagrant, from 'The Bagford Ballads'. Punishments were harsh at this period: the gallows for serious offences; the pillory, stocks, or flogging for petty misdemeanours.

This famous portrait by P. Lely of a nude lady and child is reputedly of Nell Gwyn and the infant Duke of St Albans. But another theory holds that it is of a different royal mistress—Barbara Palmer, later Duchess of Cleveland.

Theatreland was another centre of crime. Given the conditions of the time, this was inevitable; it was inevitable too that many of the offenders should be from the upper strata of society. To the looser elements of the nobility the bodies of comely actresses were a perquisite that was theirs by right, and they were always ready to shed blood in defence of their actual or potential property. Their rank made them virtually immune from legal retribution, and their habit of going about with gangs of attendant thugs helped them to get their way.

Their victims might be rivals of their own class, or they might be actors who were themselves the lovers, in some cases the husbands, of the female prey. Occasionally they were the actresses themselves. Beck Marshall of the Theatre Royal, a spirited lady, lived in fear of Sir Hugh Middleton until she had the temerity to complain to the King. Middleton lay in wait for her with one of his bravos, who assaulted her in the street, beat her up, smeared ordure on her face and put her to flight.

The actors themselves were in general a turbulent and raffish collection of men, and the Covent Garden area became a byword for brawling and lawlessness. But it was the aristocrats who set the tone. An actor was not worthy of a nobleman's sword. When Edward Kynaston offended the ineffable Sir Charles Sedley, the courtier set his hired servants to beat him up.

Such were the conditions in London, as in other parts of the country, in the absence of any effective police. In the vacuum that existed the soldiery had their part to play; but for political reasons it was a limited part. There was a deep-rooted prejudice among the freedom-loving people of England against anything that savoured of military rule; a 'standing army', associated in the popular mind with despotism as personified by Philip II of Spain or Louis XIV of France, was a spectre of horror to the seventeenth-century Englishman. Therefore Charles II, who was in fact the creator of the British Army that has existed since his time, had to use the utmost caution in his use of an instrument of the unpopularity of which he was fully

6

aware. It was permissible to call out the troops to deal with political incidents such as the Venner rising of 1661; there was indeed no other way of coping with them. But when it came to straightforward crime, on however great a scale, any use of soldiers was liable to meet the united opposition of the populace, who would side with the most brutal criminals rather than with the hated redcoats.

This feeling had of course been intensified by the years of civil war and the military dictatorship that had followed. Cromwell's major-generals had not endeared themselves to the people over whom they had been set to rule.

Nor was this general dislike of the military without justification. The fear that King Charles might be designing to create what would now be called a police state, such as had undoubtedly existed in the 1650s, was quite unfounded; he never showed any inclination in that direction. But the conduct of the troops was, more often than not, deplorable. Soldiers were recruited, in many cases, from the criminal classes of the population; and the possession of arms and uniform merely enabled them to pursue their normal way of life with greater ease. Drunkenness was almost universal. On one occasion a trooper of the Life Guards shot a barmaid who was slow in serving him with brandy. As to the officers, some were efficient and conscientious. But commissions were held by place-seekers around the court, men of the stamp of Sedley and Buckhurst, who cared nothing for the discipline of the troops under their command and looked on their rank simply as an extra source of income. Such an army was hardly calculated to inspire that respect in the civil population without which a police force cannot operate.

Yet on occasions the troops did act in a police capacity, and not always without effect. Infantry garrisons were placed in towns spaced throughout England, and companies could be, and were, called out from time to time to deal with particularly severe outbreaks of crime in the neighbouring countryside. Their very presence helped to preserve some standard of law and order, for the most lawless of robbers might well be afraid of soldiers with arms in their hands, however akin those soldiers might be to them in spirit.

The formation of a standing army, in defiance of popular prejudices, was one of the achievements of the restored monarch. As the recent work of Dr John Childs on the subject has shown, it was a new creation; the continuous history of the British Army dates from the early years of the Restoration. In previous ages armed forces had been raised as required in times of crisis, and this improvisation had acquired a new dimension during the Civil Wars. The most efficient instrument of war then forged was unquestionably the New Model Army raised by the Parliamentarians in 1645 and commanded by Sir Thomas Fairfax. It had won the Battle of Naseby which ensured the final defeat of Charles I, reached its pitch of perfection in the Second Civil War, and then remained in being as the mainstay and bulwark of the Cromwellian dictatorship. It can thus be regarded as the first standing army to be maintained in England in time of peace.

The New Model, however, was totally disbanded in 1660, with the exception of a few garrison companies, the regiments of the Dukes of York and Gloucester, and those commanded by the Duke of Albemarle. When King Charles II formed his own army, he started afresh from scratch.

The disbandment of the New Model meant that the trained bands were the sole military force in the kingdom apart from those few regular units left in being. Such had been the position before the Great Civil War; the trained bands, the 'militia', civilian volunteers who were given some military training and could be mustered in time of emergency, were considered adequate for national defence. But times had changed. The Civil Wars, in which the trained bands had played a considerable and in some cases extremely efficient part on both sides, had created a new outlook on martial matters. Charles II decided that he must have an army of his own.

It was his own sole responsibility. One of the prime points

of contention between Charles I and his rebellious subjects had been the matter of control of the militia; the monarch's opponents had propounded the revolutionary doctrine that such control belonged to the Parliament. They had won the day then, but the Restoration had changed all that. Under the Militia Act of 1661 the old system was restored whereby management of national defence and the armed forces was the prerogative of the King alone.

In its first form the new army was a small ceremonial establishment, designed to guard the King's person and to provide a military presence on state occasions. Modelled as it was on the personal guard of Louis XIV, it consisted of four regiments: the Life Guards, the Royal Horse Guards, and the first and second Foot Guards; the last in the list was General Monk's own regiment, the Coldstream Guards, specifically exempted from the disbandment of the New Model.

As time went on new regiments were formed and the King's guard became a genuine army. The acquisition of Tangier, part of the dowry of King Charles's Portuguese queen, meant additional recruitment, for the new territory needed a substantial garrison. For the necessary manpower there were various sources of supply. Officers and men of the New Model, trained soldiers now out of work, formed a nucleus. Returned Royalist officers who had fought on the Continent in the Thirty Years War, mainly in Flanders, supplied a further element of military experience. Many members of the trained bands, at least partially used to bearing arms, were willing to join a regular force. Lastly there were the multitude of impoverished citizens, largely down-and-outs and criminals, who were attracted by the pay (such as it was), the luxury of carrying good weapons, and the prospect of free drink. It was these who gave the army so evil a name; but numbers could not have been kept up without them.

The army was the creation of King Charles II; but its administration was in the highly capable hands of George Monk Duke of Albemarle. As Lord General he was in sole and undisputed command. Just as in the years after Waterloo the management of the British Army was almost exclusively in the hands of the Duke of Wellington, so the Army of the Restoration was indebted for all that it achieved to the Duke of Albemarle. It was he who judiciously weeded out the dissidents from among the former members of the New Model, thus minimizing the chances of sedition within; who welded the disparate elements into a more or less harmonious whole; and who worked out the chain of command and the details of organization in a new and by no means orderly force. Charles II's army had grave shortcomings, but in spite of its ill-discipline and its lawless element it fulfilled its function by no means discreditably. That it did so was due above all to George Monk.

Somewhat apart from the army, being indeed of an inter-service nature, lay the important organism known as the Ordnance, which controlled the supply of weapons, particularly gunpowder, cannon and small guns, and whose powers had the constitutional effect of separating the services from their arms. The Board of Ordnance was older than any permanent military organization, its origins having been traced as far back as the thirteenth century; the first known Master of the Ordnance was appointed in 1414.

In the years which followed the Restoration, the Ordnance reached the height of its influence. Its responsibilities included giving defence advice to the Privy Council, with the inventoried ownership of all arms by land and sea before, during and after service. The Board of Ordnance controlled the appointment of all gunners and engineers, ashore and afloat; acquired in 1667 the responsibility for defence fortifications; organized amphibious expeditions; sponsored science and industry; and placed its own notes of credit in the money market.

The Master-General of the Ordnance, or when this office was in commission the Lieutenant-General, was a power in the land. For ten years after 1660 the Lieutenant-General of the Ordnance was Sir William Legge, staunchest of Royalist officers, who had been the closest friend and ally of Prince Rupert in the days of the Civil War and after. Legge was the soul of honour, and under him the Ordnance Office curbed the scale of corruption; the trouble, however, was too deep-rooted for him to cure. At the time of the Dutch wars England's admirals were full of complaints about the supply of arms and ammunition.

In the 1660s the Ordnance was concerned more with the navy than the army because the navy had bigger guns. But it amounted in a sense to a third service, standing half-way between, and to some extent above, the other two. The partnership between the Navy and Ordnance Boards was the most potent link joining the army to the navy, and co-ordinating the fighting style of both.

The navy was without question the pre-eminent service at the time of the Restoration. In this period, as in all others before the development of air strategy, the defence of an island kingdom depended on sea-power. And the senior service could boast a far longer history than any English regular army.

In a sense there had been an English navy since the early Middle Ages. The Viking invasions had necessitated counter-measures; Alfred the Great had not only built up a substantial fleet but had trained a body of fighting sailors to man it. Thereafter his successors had found it necessary to maintain ships and crews to fight off the threat of foreign invasion and to protect English trade. English aggressive action too had demanded naval support; when medieval kings embarked on Continental ventures, as in the Hundred Years War for instance, transports were needed to take the feudal levies, raised *ad hoc*, to their destination.

This is not to say that most of the monarchs of these earlier ages had maintained very much of a fleet. The general practice was to commandeer merchant vessels, armed for their own protection, as circumstances demanded, and to use their crews as temporary servants of the crown. This system was paramount at least as late as the reign of Elizabeth I, whose

martial achievements at sea could not have been achieved
without the assistance of privateers such as Drake and Hawkins.

It is thus impossible to ascribe even an approximate date
to the foundation of the Royal Navy, or to point to any one
sovereign as its creator. Alfred certainly has a claim, and so
has Henry VIII, who expanded the naval forces of the crown
from half a dozen ships to several score, and equipped them with
guns of the latest pattern, a comparatively new feature in the
early sixteenth century: the *Great Harry* was the finest warship
of its time.

What can be said is that the Royal Navy, as opposed to
forces improvised in time of war, had a recognized history by
the beginning of the seventeenth century. It was an institution
in which the English took conscious pride. The prejudice
against a standing army was never extended to a standing navy.

Yet the navy in anything like the form in which we know it
today was the creation of the Stewarts. James I, a man of peace,
took little interest in it; but his son brought a new dimension
to the whole question. The problem in his time was mainly
that of bringing order to the English Channel, over which the
English kings traditionally claimed sovereignty and which
was now the prey of corsairs and pirates, some of them coming
from as far away as Algiers. To counter this menace Charles I
built a great new fleet, and to finance its construction and its
manning he extended the imposition of 'ship money', the tax
paid by the maritime counties for the defence of the realm, to
inland areas. This measure in 1635 led to discontent which
is regarded as one of the causes of the Great Civil War,
though its extent has been exaggerated; but it enabled the
King to create a naval force which far excelled any that had
existed before. The *Sovereign of the Seas*, the pride of the
fleet, was one of the largest and most beautiful warships afloat.

Charles I was denied time to make much use of the fleet
thus created, and when the Civil War broke out it quickly
fell into the hands of his enemies; this was one of the most
potent causes of the Roundhead victory. And when Cromwell

came to power the naval force built up by King Charles served
him in good stead. With the help of such competent admirals
as Blake, Lawson, Monk and Penn, he swept the Channel of
privateers, asserted English supremacy in the narrow seas,
and embarked on the mainly successful First Dutch War.
In doing so he piled up formidable debts for the restored
monarch.

The Restoration, however, saw the greatest advance in the
naval establishment. Charles II took the closest interest in his
fleet. He had commanded, in the Second Civil War, that part
of it which adhered to the Royalist cause, and, in his teens
as he was, had proved himself a competent and self-reliant
admiral. He had a detailed knowledge of naval architecture, and
delighted to watch over the minutiae of technical development.
In his hands, and in those of his brother James who took up
his post of Lord High Admiral at the Restoration, the ship-
money fleet of Charles I was developed and expanded.

The navy was the chief agent of Charles II's trade policy.
In 1660 the Commonwealth's Navigation Act was re-enacted
and brought up to date, laying down that goods must be
imported either in English ships or vessels of the country of
origin, and protecting colonial trade from foreign competition.
England's principal rivals in trade and at sea were still the
Dutch, and Restoration legislation was aimed first and foremost
at Dutch power and aggression.

Expansion of the navy was continuous in the 1660s. Money
as always was short, but the rising population enabled recruiting
to the fleet to be maintained, and the development of trade
made it possible to build new ships of the latest design. In
all this the King and the Duke of York were the moving
spirits; as the period went on they acquired the assistance of
a hard-working and capable subordinate in the young Samuel
Pepys, whose name has rightly been associated with the
expansion of the Restoration navy.

The navy thus bore a totally different aspect from that of
the army. This being so, it is somewhat curious that, at least

where the higher command was concerned, there was still no recognition of the distinction between land and sea warfare. When the time came the Restoration threw up some first-class commanders at sea, but most of them were soldiers first and sailors only second, and their tactical conceptions were based on military notions. The Duke of York's martial experience had been almost entirely military, and so was that of the Duke of Albemarle, though he had served at sea under Cromwell. Prince Rupert had plenty of knowledge of maritime matters, acquired in his semi-privateering exploits during the interregnum; but his reputation was based on his cavalry leadership in the First Civil War.

The military nature of seventeenth-century warfare was reflected in the composition of fleets of the period. They were composed mainly of quantities of small vessels which were often at the mercy of wind and weather. Tactical control was reduced to the simplest rules and was based on military principles.

Yet times were gradually changing. Fighting Instructions were issued by the Commonwealth 'generals-at-sea' which laid down the principles of naval warfare, and these were reissued with improvements by the Duke of York in 1665. The development of gunnery during the previous hundred years or so led to the introduction of the line-ahead system, in which each ship, sailing parallel with the enemy, could employ its full fire-power in broadside. Seventeenth-century warships, tall and stalwart vessels of seldom more than 1,000 tons, were classified in 'rates' according to the number of guns they carried—from first-rates of eighty guns or more to sixth-rates of fewer than twelve.

The men who manned these ships were drawn from most walks of life. As in the army, commissions were often given to scions of noble families with little aptitude for their chosen profession; but other officers were experienced seamen who had risen from the lower deck either in the navy or in merchant vessels. In the years to come this question of 'gentlemen captains' and 'tarpaulins' was thrashed out in the service and in the council chamber until a reasonably unified corps of officers with sea experience was established. The Duke of York took an important step when in 1661 he issued an order that a proportion of 'such young gentlemen as are willing to apply themselves to the learning of navigation, and fitting themselves for the service of the sea' should serve a term as midshipmen, with the training that this implied. Henceforth high birth was not to be equated with ignorance of naval life.

Among the ordinary seamen there were likewise many with genuine experience and talent. A substantial nucleus was formed by the sailors of the Commonwealth still serving in the ships, and there was steady recruitment from the merchant service. The pay was attractive. Seamen were paid 19s to 24s a month, all found: good money in the seventeenth century, though a sailor once in the service was apt to find that his pay was usually in arrears. Finally there was the press-gang. In time of war or crisis any unoffending young man who could not prove himself indispensable in civilian life was liable to be seized by the authorities and forced to serve his country in arms. The press-gang affected the army too, but in practice it was used only for manning overseas garrisons such as that of Tangier.

Once aboard one of His Majesty's vessels, the sailor, pressed or otherwise, found himself subject to the strictest discipline. Flogging was inflicted for the slightest of offences, and the death penalty was not infrequently inflicted. 'Nothing but hanging will man the fleet,' wrote Sir William Coventry. Life was one of continual hardship and the roughest conditions; rations meagre and often virtually inedible.

Yet these disparate elements, living a life afloat that was anything but enviable, managed to weld themselves into a service of which both they and their compatriots were proud. Sailors ashore were a byword; in any port in which they were let loose they drank, raped and rioted; brawling was the normal order of the day. But in action at sea these men came into their own. They met their test in the Dutch wars and were not found wanting. There was frequent petty indiscipline, and mutinies on a larger scale were not unknown; but the English navy held its own against the more professional service of the Dutch.

Here was another difference between the two services. The army had little but garrison duties to perform at this time, but the navy was a genuine fighting force. In bearing the brunt of what warfare there was in the Restoration period, it worked out its own salvation and developed a sea tradition which took it further and further from the military system.

The sailors of Charles II's reign were a rip-roaring set of men, apt to spread panic among the peaceful population of seaside towns. But in time of war they won respect. Dryden wrote of them after the Four Days Fight in the Second Dutch War:

Thousands were there in darker fame that dwell,
Whose deeds some nobler poem shall adorn:
And, though to me unknown, they sure fought well
Whom Rupert led, and who were British born.

The character of the British sailor has not noticeably changed through the centuries.

Religion

The Church is grown so overstock'd of late,
That if you walk abroad, you hardly meet
More Porters now than Parsons in the street.
At every corner they are forc'd to ply
For Jobs of hawkering Divinity:
And half the number of the Sacred Herd
Are fain to stroll, and wander unpreferr'd.

John Oldham

'When I mention religion, I mean the Christian religion; and not only the Christian religion, but the Protestant religion; and not only the Protestant religion, but the Church of England.'

Mr Thwackum flourished some three-quarters of a century after the Restoration, but his sentiments may be taken as typical of many, probably the majority, of those Anglican clergymen who came back into their own in 1660. The conception that forms of belief other than one's own might have a right to equality of expression had not as yet made much headway. The Church of England was in power once more, and it claimed a monopoly of the truth as certainly as did other creeds when their adherents found themselves in the same position.

This is not to say that Christianity in whatever form it might assume was not regarded as having an innate superiority to all other religions. In the eyes of the Church of England Presbyterians, Quakers, even papists, however regrettable their errors, were at least closer to divine revelation than the 'lesser breeds without the Law' who did not accept that Christ was God Incarnate. Advocates of toleration of all creeds (and they were few indeed) never suggested that such toleration should be extended to the heathen or the atheist. The question, however,

hardly arose as a matter of practical debate, since England in
the seventeenth century was almost exclusively Christian.

Not only was the country Christian, but religion dominated
the life of every man and woman to an extent difficult to realize
today. A man might or might not take an interest in national
politics, which were outside the purview of the average
individual; he might have to play a part in local affairs, which
he probably regarded as a burden to be avoided if possible; he
might, but in most cases did not, concern himself with the art or
literature of the day; but religion was an integral part of his
life. He went to church every Sunday as a matter of course, and
it was there that he learned the news of the day so far as it
concerned him. The newspapers that had flourished so vigorously during the Civil Wars had entered upon a period of
decline. There was only the official *London Gazette*, which had
a limited circulation among the educated classes. Such items as
it was important for all to know were given by the bishops to the
parish clergy, who in turn read them out from the pulpit to
their congregations. It was the parish priest, or the nonconformist pastor, who laid down the rules of life for the
individual and the family; who told them how they must
behave and what they must do for the good of their souls.

Above all there was the Bible, the influence of which was
immense. Every parishioner was accustomed to hearing
sonorous phrases of the Authorized Version read out in his
local church. Everyone who could read at all read the Bible; in
innumerable cases it was the only book he ever did read. And
those whose education had not progressed so far listened to the
Word and knew long passages by heart. Pepys when walking
on Epsom Downs came upon 'the most pleasant and innocent
sight': an old shepherd, 'the most like one of the old Patriarchs
that ever I saw in my life', and 'his little boy reading, far from
any houses or sight of people, the Bible to him.'

Just as virtually all Englishmen were Christians, so were
they all fundamentalists. Holy Scripture was paramount, and
the Bible story was accepted as literally true, historically as well

as theologically. Eminent scholars had worked out, by a process
of pure deduction, that the world had been created in the year
4004 BC, and acceptance of this date was common to all sects.
Hence proceeded the sequence of events as revealed in the Old
and New Testaments, the accuracy of which it occurred to none
to call in question.

Here all were agreed. It was in interpretation of the
frequently obscure words of Holy Writ, and in working out
therefrom the details of church government and authority, that
all the deep and bitter differences that bedevilled the Christian
religion in the seventeenth century had arisen. In the Middle
Ages all interpretation was in the hands of the Universal
Church, and despite periodical outbreaks of heresy the judgement of Rome had been in general accepted, in England as in
other nations of Christendom. But when Henry VIII cast off
the authority of the Pope the way was opened to private
judgement, and as time went on this judgement became more
and more diffuse and the Bible was subjected to countless
different interpretations.

These differences reached a climax in the seventeenth
century, with the development of Puritanism and the multiplication of new sects. The excesses to which private judgement
attained were depicted by Dryden with his usual devastating
clarity, if from the biased viewpoint of a staunch Anglican (this
was before his ultimate change of faith). In *Religio Laici* he
wrote:

> The Book thus put in every vulgar hand,
> Which each presum'd he best Cou'd understand,
> The Common Rule was made the common Prey;
> And at the mercy of the Rabble lay.
> The tender Page with horny Fists was gaul'd;
> And he was gifted most that loudest baul'd;
> The spirit gave the Doctoral Degree,
> And every member of a Company
> Was of his Trade and of the Bible free.

Plain Truths enough for needfull use they found;
But men wou'd still be itching to expound;
Each was ambitious of th' obscurest place,
No measure ta'n from Knowledge, all from Grace.

This proliferation of sects and of Biblical interpretations, though not a peculiarly English phenomenon, had developed with particular intensity owing to the course that English history had taken. When Henry VIII broke away from Rome he had no thought of founding a Protestant church on the German model. He had himself denounced Martin Luther in his *Assertio Septem Sacramentorum*, the work that gained him from Pope Leo X the title of Defender of the Faith; and despite the schism he had created he remained faithful to the end of his life to the essentials of the Catholic faith. The break with Rome had been the outcome of his own domestic affairs; the last thing he intended was the initiation of a doctrinal revolution.

Nevertheless he made that revolution inevitable. By suppressing the monasteries and distributing among his more powerful subjects such of their wealth as he did not keep for himself, he gave the magnates so enriched a vested interest in seeing that no return to monastic influence could take place. The spread of Protestant doctrines was the best guarantee against a resurgence of ecclesiastical power, and so, in the next reign when the magnates came into their own, the Reformation took possession of England. Just as the Protestant princes of Germany furthered the revolt engendered by Martin Luther's defiance of Rome, so the great landowners who wielded power in the name of the boy-king Edward VI encouraged the growth of Lutheranism and Calvinism in England. And after the jolt inflicted by the Catholic reaction under Mary I, the process was accelerated.

The Elizabethan settlement in religion aimed at comprehensiveness within the now restored Church of England. The tastes of Elizabeth I herself inclined towards what would in due course be called the High Church. She favoured order and ritual which were the ecclesiastical equivalent of the stately etiquette that surrounded her court, and emphasized her own position of Supreme Governor of the Church. The elastic nature of the settlement, however, was designed to include within the structure of the Church all forms of Christian thought which had agreed in casting off the authority of Rome. Thus the Puritan movement, which gathered force during the closing years of the sixteenth century, was at first a movement within the Church of England.

To define Puritanism is not easy. Richard Baxter, the movement's most eminent representative at the time of the Restoration, saw the essential characteristics of a Puritan as a serious effort to live a godly life and a desire to achieve further reformation in the Church. Such a definition, however, could apply to any good Christian who was prepared to cast a critical eye on the ecclesiastical establishment. The Puritans went further than this. What particularly characterized them as time went on, and in the seventeenth century drove them into non-conformity, was a refusal to recognize the administrative structure of the Elizabethan settlement, and especially the institution of episcopacy which was the legacy of the Catholic Church.

Episcopacy was the cornerstone of the royal supremacy. 'No Bishop, no King,' was the dictum of James I, who in general was not unsympathetic towards Puritanism. And so Puritanism came to be associated with revolt against the crown, and as the country moved towards civil war, a conflict which was at least half a religious conflict, the extreme Protestant sects proceeded to break away from the established church.

The personalities of the monarchs played a conspicuous part in the process. King James, the son of Catholic parents, had been brought up as a Calvinist in his native Scotland. In his youth he was subjected to insults and humiliations from the abominable John Knox and the Presbyterian elders; but he imbibed the principles of the Presbyterian creed, and so far as he committed himself intellectually to any one set of beliefs it was to what might be called the left wing of Protestantism. At the same time he looked with a kind of nostalgic affection towards the ancestral Church of Rome, and he would if he could have softened the harsh penal laws enacted against his Catholic subjects. When he came into his larger kingdom, the Church of England was something new in his practical experience, though as an accomplished theologian he knew all about it in theory. It attracted him greatly as an institution that supported his own kingly authority, and he performed his duties as Supreme Governor with zest; but he had no wish to impose its doctrines on those unwilling to subscribe to them. With his own inclination towards ultra-Protestantism, and his partly subconscious leanings towards Catholicism, he yearned to bring all shades of thought under his own benevolent wing. Persecution was alien to his nature; he preferred persuasion by discussion and debate to autocratic dictatorship. In Church as in State his aim was to 'win all men's hearts'.

So it was that in the reign of the first Stewart king ecclesiastical dissension, though it was all the time maturing under the surface, did not come to a head. It was different under his successor. Charles I was as convinced an Anglican as ever lived; his church was even dearer to him than his crown, as he was to prove in the last stages of his tragic life. Calvinism, Puritanism, ultra-Protestantism, had no appeal for him; and under his rule the Anglican creed moved inexorably further in the direction of an exclusively sacramental, or High Church, position. Ritual and liturgical ceremony became the order of the day, and King Charles set his stamp on the process by his appointment, in 1633, of William Laud, Bishop of London, to the Archbishopric of Canterbury.

Laud was, to his opponents at least, the epitome of High-Churchmanship, and in the view of Protestant activists the reforms which he initiated were designed to lead England back into the Catholic fold. In fact he was not a Romanizer; for all his love of ceremonial he was as much opposed to papal authority as he was to what seemed to him the anarchical aims of Puritanism. What he wanted was order and decency in the rites and administration of the church; dignity in its service and discipline in its administration, with the bishops in full authority under the King. In Laud's programme the royal supremacy was all-important and must be defended as much from Roman as from Low Church encroachments.

Thus when the great struggle between King and Parliament broke out in England it took the form, in its ecclesiastical aspects, of a revolt against the Church of England, associated in the Protestant mind with Laudianism and the royal supremacy, and in the ultimate issue with Roman supremacy. The Puritan sects, hitherto owning allegiance, however tenuous, to the established church, were now openly nonconformist; and when the war ended in victory for the anti-Royalist faction, the Church of England itself became a church in exile.

Multiplication of sects was in these circumstances inevitable. In Parliament indeed, largely under the influence of the Roundheads' Scottish allies, Presbyterianism was at least as authoritarian a system as was Anglican episcopacy; no bishop was ever more dictatorial than an elder of the Kirk. So, just as the opening stages of the Civil War involved a rebellion against Anglicanism, so its later developments brought a second revolt against Presbyterianism.

It was in the New Model Army, the organ of final victory for the Roundheads, the force which brought Cromwell to supreme power in England, that the variety of sects known collectively as Independents flourished. The Army's Commander-in-Chief was Thomas Fairfax, himself a Presbyterian; but its religious inspiration came from Cromwell. In the early days of the conflict Cromwell, then a junior officer but with a keen military eye, detected the weakness of the Roundhead troops. The Cavaliers were men of quality and of honour, pledged to serve their king; whereas their opponents were 'old decayed serving-men, and tapsters and such kind of fellows', with no ideal to fight for. So, when he rose to influence as a trainer of troops, he set himself to provide them with one. The ideal was that of religion, and Cromwell strove to inspire his men with his own Puritan fervour, representing the Cavaliers as papists and sinners whom it was the duty of the shock-troops of God to destroy.

At the same time he did not lay down for them the obligation to follow any one particular brand of Puritanism. And so in this most intensely religious of armies, which eventually found itself the paramount power in the land, countless varieties of thought, Dryden's 'numerous host of dreaming sects', came into being. There were Socinians and Anabaptists, Deists and Quakers, Fifth Monarchy Men and Seventh Day Adventists, with many others whose names have faded into oblivion. They were united only in hostility to Anglicanism, Presbyterianism and the Church of Rome.

When Cromwell came to power, as he did soon after the end of the Great Civil War, all these sects were given full play. In 1653 he drove out the Rump Parliament and called a new assembly of nominated members drawn from the ranks of the Independent congregations; this was soon nicknamed the Barebone Parliament after one of its members who rejoiced in the characteristically Puritan name of Praise-God Barebone. A few months later Cromwell, never a patient man with parliaments, sent this one packing and assumed dictatorial powers as Protector, governing with his Council of State.

Cromwell, himself the accepted leader of the Independents, was personally inclined towards toleration, though he never extended it to Catholics. In the climate of the time there could be no question of a return to influence of the Church of England, which was outlawed but not actively persecuted; but all forms of what in the future would constitute nonconformity were given freedom of worship.

Such, broadly speaking, was the situation which prevailed until the Restoration, though in the unsettled conditions that followed Oliver Cromwell's death Anglican practices began to creep back. When it became at first probable, and then certain, that the monarchy would return, this process was accelerated;

and when the Rump was recalled, in May 1659, Presbyterianism also raised its head once more.

The return of the King meant, of course, the return of the Church of England; and with the resurgence of Anglicanism the lines were drawn more firmly than they had ever been drawn before. There was now no question of any form of Puritanism other than Presbyterianism remaining as a movement within the Church of England; members of the various sects were nonconformists or 'dissenters', unqualified to receive the privileges and the state support which were the prerogative of the established church.

That church itself, in its higher echelons at least, tended towards the form of the High Anglicanism practised by Charles I and Laud; that is to say, towards ritualism and sacramentalism. Hyde was an uncompromising High Churchman, and it was Hyde who was the moving spirit of the new ecclesiastical settlement. He was fully supported by the bishops. The comprehensiveness that had been the ideal aimed at by Elizabeth I and James I was not altogether abandoned; what were to become known as the Low Church and the Broad Church, with their lesser emphasis on the sacraments, were still accepted within the fold, accepting episcopacy as they did. But such schools of thought had no influence in high quarters. Thus the gulf between the Church of England and the nonconformist congregations was accentuated.

The great point of issue in 1660 was therefore how far toleration should go; what degree of latitude should be allowed to those who refused their assent to the doctrine and discipline of the Church of England as by law established. First, however, the church had to re-establish its own order. Cathedrals and churches, allowed to fall into decay and devoted to all sorts of secular uses during the interregnum, were restored as quickly as possible to their old condition. The traditional order of service and the use of the Book of Common Prayer were brought back, and nonconformist incumbents (unless they were prepared to change their ways and conform) were ejected in favour of

orthodox clergymen, some of them introduced for the first time
and some restored to the cures over which they had presided
before the times of trouble.

It was necessary also to appoint a chief pastor for the
restored Church of England. The see of Canterbury had been
vacant since the death of Archbishop Laud. After four years of
imprisonment the chief enemy of the Puritans had, in 1645,
perished at their hands, beheaded at the Tower of London. Now
a successor had to be found, and there was one obvious choice.
William Juxon, as Bishop of London, had been Laud's right-
hand man. He had been an intimate friend and admirer of King
Charles I, and as such had been permitted to attend his sovereign
on the scaffold. After that he was left unmolested and allowed to
live in peace and retirement in Gloucestershire. He was now
seventy-seven years old and in feeble health; but the veneration
in which he was held made him the only possible candidate in
the eyes of the Anglican community. He was a saintly man, mild
in manner and tolerant in disposition. He was accordingly
appointed to the vacant Archbishopric of Canterbury, and for
three years before his death held the office of Primate of All
England; but owing to the frail state of his health he made
hardly a pretence of carrying out his duties, and he took no part
in working out the details of the new settlement. The one
important ecclesiastical ceremony in which he took part was the
coronation of Charles II, and then he collapsed before the end.

His work was in fact carried out by the new Bishop of London,
Gilbert Sheldon, who in 1663 was to succeed him at Canterbury.
Sheldon had all the vigour that Juxon lacked. A man of sixty-
two at the time of the Restoration, he too had been in attendance
on King Charles during the time of his captivity. He had then
and thereafter imbibed a fierce enmity towards all forms of
Puritanism, and he stood forth now as a staunch upholder of
High Church Anglicanism and an opponent of concessions to
nonconformity.

Hyde and Sheldon were the prime movers in the vital
discussions which were now to take place on relations between

the Church of England and the Puritans. There was, however, a third figure on the establishment side whose views could not be discounted. This was the King, holder of the official titles of Supreme Governor of the Church and Defender of the Faith. By no manner of means could King Charles be regarded as a religious man. The Anglican Church in its doctrinal aspects meant little to him. He attended its services and took part in its ceremonial as his royal duty required him to do, but he mocked at the discourse of pious divines and was apt to go to sleep during sermons. 'My Lord, my lord,' a preacher is reported to have protested to a somnolent peer, 'you snore so loud you will wake the King.' When it came to church appointments he was inclined to give preferment to a man who could make him laugh rather than to one renowned for learning or piety.

There was, however, one thing that King Charles did care about. This was religious toleration. Almost alone except for his brother James, he wanted all his subjects to be allowed to worship God in any way they chose. In this he was following the tradition of his family. James I had not been a persecutor, and had it not been for the fatal folly of the Gunpowder Plot at the very beginning of his reign his tolerance would probably have gone further than it did. Charles I, for all his belief in the absolute rightness of Anglican doctrine, looked with a kindly eye on those from whom he differed. In the years of his personal rule he did what he could to soften the severity of the penal laws, and when Monsignor George Con, a cultured Scot who won his friendship, was in England as papal agent, he even took tentative steps towards an exploration of the possibilities of a reunion between the Roman and Anglican Churches.

Charles II went still further in his views on toleration. Unlike his father and grandfather, he was a travelled man. He had lived in Calvinist Holland, Lutheran Germany, Catholic France and Presbyterian Scotland; and though his humiliating experiences in the last-named filled him with a lifelong dislike of the Presbyterian creed (no religion for a gentleman, he decided) the general effect on his character was to convince him of the absurdity and futility of trying to impose one particular set of beliefs on an entire population by physical coercion. His attitude was that of an intelligent, civilized, easy-going man of the world with no ardent religious feelings of his own. He had friends devoted to various Christian beliefs; and he saw no reason to regard a person who held views other than those that happened to be orthodox in his country as a double-dyed villain or a deliberate perverter of the truth.

When it came to his attitude to Catholics, there was a further incentive. At the time of his hunted wanderings after the defeat at Worcester he had come into contact with the underground world of priests and laymen living under the burden of the penal laws. The Penderel brothers, the humble woodcutters of Staffordshire, were a Catholic family, and they had proved themselves loyal friends to the point of heroism, risking their lives to give him shelter. When he left Boscobel for Moseley he was befriended by the Benedictine Father Huddleston, who showed him his secret oratory and hid him in the priest-hole constructed as refuge for the outlawed clergy who faced the death penalty for their faith. Standing before Father Huddleston's altar, King Charles told him that 'he knew he was a priest, and he needed not fear to own it, for if it pleased God to restore him to his kingdom, they should never more need privacies'. The hope of redeeming this pledge was always in King Charles's mind, and he never forgot the devotion of his Catholic subjects displayed towards him in his hour of need.

As regards his Protestant subjects, King Charles had given express promises of toleration. The Declaration of Breda, drawn up by Hyde in the name of the King, contained the passage: 'We do declare a liberty to tender consciences, and that no man shall be disquieted or called in question for differences of opinion in matter of religion which do not disturb the peace of the kingdom.' And to a deputation of Quakers Charles said: 'Of this you may be assured, that you shall none of you suffer for your opinions or religion, so long as you live peaceably, and you have the word of a king for it.'

The Quakers were hardly among those whose activities were regarded as not disturbing the peace of the kingdom. Founded by George Fox during the first Civil War, the Society of Friends preached pacifism, and its adherents in later ages were to become known for meekness and mildness. But in their earlier days this was not their reputation; they were out to shock their contemporaries into recognizing their virtues, and this easily led to violence. They had a penchant for taking off their clothes in public to draw attention to their preaching. One of their number toured market-places naked and smeared with dung, announcing that God would similarly besmear the followers of false religion. Another rode into Bristol on an ass while his followers strewed branches before him and proclaimed him to be Christ.

It was excesses such as these that alienated both officials and peaceful citizens from all forms of Puritanism, which became associated in the public mind with violence and lawlessness; and the climate of opinion, together with the rigid Anglicanism of the ruling party, made it hard for the King to carry out his promises of toleration. He himself, with his liberal outlook and humane intelligence, might look with an indulgent eye on the idiosyncracies of the sects. But his subjects as a whole did not; and nor did his Lord Chancellor.

The Presbyterians stood apart from the rest. A highly disciplined community, they at least could not be associated with lawless excesses. Their gravity of demeanour could not be further removed than it was from the conduct of Fifth Monarchy Men and Quakers. Moreover as a body they had been largely instrumental in bringing about the Restoration; Monk himself, though politically independent, followed the Presbyterian creed in his private worship. It was therefore hoped in some high quarters in 1660 that the Presbyterians could be included within the comprehensive system of the Church of England. Their respected leader Richard Baxter was even offered a bishopric. He refused it, but was appointed a chaplain to the King and was licensed by Sheldon to preach within the diocese of London provided he would abstain from saying anything contrary to the doctrine and discipline of the Church of England.

A few months after the Restoration a declaration was drafted in which King Charles reaffirmed the promises he had made at Breda. Liberty was accorded to 'tender consciences', and the King expressed himself ready to give his consent to any Act of Parliament that might be passed to that end. With regard to Catholics, he stated that the services they had rendered to his father and himself entitled them to favourable consideration, and that therefore he did not intend to exclude them from all benefit of the promised indulgence, though he emphasized that they must not expect complete toleration.

At the same time bishoprics were offered to three other prominent Presbyterians, as well as Baxter—Stephen Reynolds, Edmund Calamy and Thomas Manton. Reynolds accepted.

The King's declaration was welcomed by the Presbyterians, to whom it seemed unexpectedly generous. Baxter himself considered that ministers of his own persuasion could in these circumstances conform with the established church and was ready to use his influence to induce them to do so. Yet at the same time both Presbyterians and Anglicans looked with a disapproving eye on the olive branch held out to the papists.

It is not easy to account for the virulence of anti-Catholic feeling prevalent in seventeenth-century England. Partly it dated back to the Marian persecution, which even after a hundred years left bitter memories. Partly it drew its force from a typically English distrust of the foreigner. Not only was the papacy an alien power, but France and Spain, the two traditional foes of England, were Catholic nations; Spain was a fierce oppressor of Protestants, and though since the time of Henry IV France had looked on them with a tolerant eye this counted for little in the minds of Englishmen. Most of all, however, the feeling arose from sheer ignorance. Catholics were an underground body, little known to the community at large and suspected of every kind of diabolical activity. The passive harmlessness of their lives, let alone the heroism of the fugitive priests who ministered to them, did not impinge on the public consciousness. The magnates whose wealth was created from the confiscation of church property had for generations done all they could to foster the fear and hatred felt for this obscure minority of the population.

To discuss the terms of a religious settlement and the King's proposed declaration, a full-dress conference was now called at Worcester House, the residence of the Lord Chancellor. The King was present, with Hyde, Ormonde and a number of bishops. No delegates from the Independents were invited but the Presbyterians were represented by Baxter, Reynolds and Calamy.

The terms on which the Presbyterians might submit to Anglican discipline and episcopal authority were thrashed out in detail. Various concessions were offered. Bishops would accept advice from presbyters appointed to cathedral chapters; communion could be received otherwise than on bended knee; use of the surplice was not to be enjoined. Further decisions regarding church ceremonial were to be left to a national synod.

So far, so good. The Presbyterians were not dissatisfied with what was offered. But it was not they alone who were concerned. Tender consciences were not exclusively Presbyterian, and it was when it came to the matter of dissenters in general that discord arose. At the King's instance, Hyde took up the question of the various sects outside the two main denominations and the plan for toleration as expressed in the King's declaration. Petitions had been received, he said, from various Independent congregations, and in response the King proposed that: 'others should also be permitted to meet for religious worship, so be it they do it not to the disturbance of the peace; and that no justice of peace or officer disturb them.'

This was too much for the worthies of the conference. The object of the talks, in the eyes of those called to take part in them, was to decide what conditions should be imposed for the incorporation of the Presbyterians in the established church; neither party, apart from a few individuals, was interested in offering concessions to other brands of Christianity. And deep disquiet was aroused by the wording of the royal proposal; it was clear to the delegates that what the King was aiming at was some degree at least of toleration for the dreaded papists. The objections of the Presbyterians to the King's proposal were voiced by their leader. They did not advocate rigorous severity, said Baxter, but they must distinguish between tolerable and intolerable opinions; those of papists and Socinians (equivalent to Unitarians) were intolerable.

Baxter was supported by the majority of the Church of England delegates, and the conference broke up. A few days later the King's declaration was published in a watered-down form. The terms offered to the Presbyterians were set out in full, but there was complete silence on the matter of dissent in general. The clause proposed concerning toleration for tender consciences was dropped.

It was a portent of things to come, and a great disappointment for the King. It would be too much to say that he was always a man of his word, but he cared deeply about the promises he had made in the Declaration of Breda and to some individuals at the time of his own misfortunes after Worcester. Now he was prevented from fulfilling them, and it was ironic that the scene of his betrayal should be Worcester House. It was brought bitterly home to him that his authority as Supreme Governor of the Church of England was severely limited.

The Worcester House Declaration itself quickly became a dead letter. The bill to give effect to it was introduced in the House of Commons in November 1660, and a long debate took place. The Convention Parliament showed a certain reluctance to reject a document that had the personal authority of the King, and a proposal was made that the matter should be shelved and left to the new assembly that was to be called in the following year. The Anglicans in the House, however, were mostly opposed to the declaration; the concessions to the Presbyterians, they felt, went too far. In the end the vote went against the second reading of the bill, and the chance of acceptance by the Presbyterians of Anglican authority was lost.

'So there is an end of that bill,' wrote Marvell, opposed to the establishment in religion as he was in politics, 'and for those excellent things therein. We must henceforth rely only upon his Majesty's goodness, who, I must say, hath hitherto been more ready to give than we to receive.'

Before the new Parliament met, in the spring of 1661, the national synod assembled which was designed to work out England's religious settlement in detail. Baxter and his Presbyterian colleagues again attended, but the dominant figure at the conference was Gilbert Sheldon, acting as usual on behalf of Archbishop Juxon. Sheldon, as well as being Bishop of London, was Master of the Savoy Hospital, and it was at the Savoy that the talks were held. They lasted for ten weeks, but in the end no more progress was made than at Worcester House. Sheldon was an uncompromising Anglican, Baxter a rigid Presbyterian. There could be little accord between them.

In the meantime what was to become known as the Cavalier Parliament had assembled, and it was in Parliament that henceforth religious questions were to be thrashed out. The Anglicans were now in undisputed authority, and they proceeded to consolidate their victory. What followed was the passing into law of a series of bills known collectively as the Clarendon Code—'those Penal Laws,' in the words of the late George Macaulay Trevelyan, 'which broke for ever the pretensions of Puritanism to political supremacy, reduced the quantity and purified the quality of its religious influence, confined its social sphere to the middle and lower classes, and created the division of England into Church and dissent.' The Clarendon Code revised the liturgy, restored the authority of the Book of Common Prayer with alterations as laid down by the bishops, and excluded all those who did not accept its provisions.

The first bill passed was the Corporation Act. This was a

political measure by which membership of municipal corporations, which controlled the choice of parliamentary representatives, was denied to those who refused to take the sacrament according to the Anglican rite.

There followed, in 1662, the more important Act of Uniformity. This asserted the authority of the Prayer Book and defined the rites and ceremonies denial of which made men ineligible for those civil offices specified by the Corporation Act. About 1,000 clergy were expelled from their livings for refusing their assent to everything contained in the Prayer Book.

The passing of the Act of Uniformity led to one more effort on the part of King Charles to counteract the severity of Anglican bigotry. At Christmas 1662 he issued a new declaration in which he again reverted to the question of indulgence for tender consciences. He asserted his complete loyalty to the Church of England, but reminded the country of the promises he had made at Breda. And he assured his subjects

that as in the first place we have been zealous to settle the uniformity of the Church of England, in discipline, ceremony and government, and shall ever constantly maintain it; so as for what concerns the penalties upon those who (living peaceable) do not conform thereunto through scruple and tenderness of misguided conscience, but modestly and without scandal perform their devotions in their own way, we shall make it our special care so far forth as in us lies, without invading the freedom of Parliament, to incline their wisdom at this next approaching sessions to concur with us in the making of some such Act for that purpose as may enable us to exercise with a more universal satisfaction that power of dispensing which we conceive to be inherent in us.

He went on to reiterate his favourite theme: he did not see why Catholics, who had proved themselves so loyal to his father and himself, should not, so long as they lived peaceably and modestly, share in such toleration as was accorded to others.

There was of course vehement opposition. This time it was the phrase 'that power of dispensing which we conceive to be inherent in us' that was seized upon. The power to exempt individuals from the operation of Acts of Parliament had always been accepted as part of the royal prerogative. What was feared now was the extension of this privilege to embrace whole bodies of men, and in particular the Catholics. The constitutional struggle over the dispensing power, which was to play so big a part in the reign of King Charles's successor, had begun.

The declaration was immediately denounced in the Commons, and the Speaker informed the King that the House would not agree to the introduction of a bill authorizing him to use the dispensing power. A bill to this effect was then introduced in the Lords, but was defeated. Among those who spoke against it was the Earl of Clarendon. It was surprising that he should set his face against his sovereign, with whom at this time he was in complete accord in most governmental matters; but he was, after all, the accepted progenitor of the Clarendon Code, and he was not prepared to see the Act of Uniformity made a dead letter.

The King now gave way, as he habitually did when confronted with determined opposition. For the time being he abandoned his attempt to secure liberty of conscience. Toleration had been defeated, and the principal losers were the Puritans. At least part of the blame for the sufferings they endured thereafter attached to themselves, and in particular to the Presbyterians, who were fanatically opposed to accepting equality before the law if there was a danger of its being shared with papists. Baxter himself, writing later of the declaration and its aftermath, said:

Some of the Independents presumed to say that the reason why all our addresses for liberty had not succeeded, was because we did not extend it to the Papists; that, for their parts, they saw no reason why the Papists should not have liberty of worship as well as others; and that it was better for them to have it, than for all of us to go without it. But the Presbyterians still answered that the king himself might do what he pleased; and if his wisdom thought meet to give liberty to the Papists, let the Papists petition for it as we did for ours; but if it were expected that we should be forced to become petitioners for liberty to popery we should never do it, whatever be the issue; nor should it be said to be our work . . .

On the 2nd of January [1663], Mr Nye [an Independent leader] came to me, to treat about our owning the king's declaration, by returning him thanks for it; when I perceived that it was designed that we must be the desirers or procurers of it; but I told him my resolution to meddle no more in such matters, having incurred already so much hatred and displeasure in endeavouring unity. The rest of the Presbyterian ministers also had enough of it, and resolved that they would not meddle; so that Mr Nye and his brethren thought that it was partly owing to us that they missed the intending liberty. But all were averse to have anything to do with the indulgence or toleration of Papists, thinking it, at least, unfit for them.

The next stage in the formulation of the Clarendon Code was the passing, in 1664, of the first Conventicle Act. This harsh measure put a ban on meetings for religious rites other than those of the Church of England. An enactment on these lines was already in force applying specifically to Quakers, who had shown themselves especially obstreperous. It was now extended to all nonconformist activities. Any such meeting became illegal if more than five people were present other than members of the household in which it took place. Anyone over sixteen years of age caught attending was subject to the penalties prescribed under the Act: for a first offence, three months' imprisonment or a fine of £5; for a second, six months or £10; for a third, transportation for seven years to America, and death if the criminal returned before the allotted period.

The Conventicle Act might be construed as a measure of sheer vindictiveness imposed by the triumphant party; but there were political as well as religious considerations. The controversies of the early 1660s had led to a spirit of unrest among the Puritan sects, manifested in spasmodic outbreaks of violence. Not only had the Quakers been active, but soon after the Restoration the rising of the crack-brained Fifth Monarchy man Thomas Venner had seriously alarmed the authorities. In 1663 there were minor armed risings in Durham and Yorkshire. The government reacted as its Jacobean predecessor had reacted to the Gunpowder Plot in 1605.

Finally, in 1665, came the Five Mile Act, the most crippling measure yet introduced. This forbade any nonconformist minister to go within five miles of any city or corporate town unless he took an oath that he would not 'at any time endeavour any alteration of Government either in Church or State'. Few of them were willing to take such an oath, and the result was that dissenting congregations, which were mainly centred in the towns, were cut off from their own ministers, on whom they depended not only for religious services but for education.

The Clarendon Code was rigorously enforced. Justices of the Peace, to whom its operation was principally entrusted, performed their duties zealously, hunting down holders of conventicles, employing paid informers, trapping ministers who strayed too near the forbidden towns. They were spurred on to their work by the clergy, under the leadership of Sheldon, now Archbishop of Canterbury, who displayed his persecuting fervour in his instructions to the clergy. In a circular letter to the bishops he wrote:

I advise that all and every of the said ecclesiastical judges and officers, and every of the clergy of your diocese, and the churchwardens of every parish by their respective ministers

Edward Hyde, first Earl of Clarendon, after A. Hanneman. As Lord Chancellor, he was a central figure of Charles II's administration, and at this period the real ruler of the kingdom.

Quakers Emigrating, from 'The Bagford Ballads'. The Clarendon Code.

be desired in their respective stations and places that they take notice of all Nonconformists, holders, frequenters, maintainers, abettors of conventicles and unlawful assemblies under pretence of religious worship, especially of the teachers and preachers in them and of places wherein the same are held, ever keeping a more watchful eye on the cities and great towns from whence the mischief is for the most part derived into the lesser villages and hamlets: and whereinsoever they find such wilful offenders that they with a hearty affection to the worship of God, the honour of the king and his laws, and the peace of the Church and kingdom, they do address themselves to the civil magistrate, justices, and others concerned, imploring their help and assistance for preventing and suppressing the same, according to the late said Act in that behalf made and set forth.

The Anglican triumph was complete. Henceforth the bishops of the Church of England ruled the country in its spiritual aspects, and the gentry hastened to conform. The upper classes were now, even more than before, overwhelmingly Anglican in sentiment and practice; eager to take advantage of the privileges accorded. Public money was available, and the clergy flourished. There was no lack of recruits; the clerical calling was once again a source of income for the younger sons of influential families, who found plenty of lucrative benefices ready to hand. In due course the profession became overcrowded; later in the reign the poet John Oldham, Dryden's protégé, complained that there were more parsons than porters in the street. The golden age of the Vicar of Bray had dawned.

There was real gain in all this. The Church of England, which in the early years of the century had been feeling its way amid determined opposition, was now able to set its house in order. Complacency and indifference to the sufferings of those without the law were one side of the coin; on the other were the development of dignity and beauty of worship that were the peculiar work of the restored Church of England. The High

7

Church ritualists were in the ascendent, and aesthetically their influence was entirely beneficial.

The upper-class nature of the establishment also conferred its benefits. The Anglican ministry became inseparably associated with the gentry. Culture and good manners were paramount, and eventually there emerged one of the pleasantist types that any church could boast: the antiquarian country parson, placid and scholarly, kind-hearted and loved by all, pottering unambitiously about his parish and making a real contribution in his study of local history and folk-lore to the sum total of academic knowledge.

For the Puritans the Clarendon Code was a tragedy. It was not to be compared with the major religious persecutions of history, but the oppression was real. Nonconformist bodies were forced into poverty and hardship, and in many cases much worse. The prisons were filled with victims of the Conventicle and Five Mile Acts; one who continually suffered was the indomitable, untutored John Bunyan, who used his periods of incarceration to produce literature that would have its message for countless generations unborn, with his visions of Doubting Castle and the Delectable Mountains.

Any follower of the various sects might suffer. Illegal meetings were dispersed by troops, and stray passers-by who had merely stopped to listen were often brutally beaten by the soldiers and thrown into the local gaol. Trials were sometimes fair but more often not. It all depended on the character of the justice concerned. In many cases, perhaps the majority, he was uninterested in evidence and merely disapproved of the opinions of the accused, who could not hope for acquittal.

The Catholics likewise lost their chance of better times. They remained an outlawed community, living quietly and unobtrusively, hoping only to be let alone, but feared and distrusted and made the scapegoats for every national calamity. The hatred felt for them would erupt in the next decade into the frenzied hysteria of the Popish Plot canard.

Toleration for 'tender consciences' had been defeated.

Charles II tried again in later years, but the opposing forces were too much for him; and he always knew when to withdraw. It was left to his brother and successor to try to impose liberty of conscience on his subjects by royal decree. It quickly cost him his throne.

The New Age

Me-thinks already, from this Chymick flame,
I see a City of more precious mold:
Rich as the Town which gives the Indies *name,*
With Silver pav'd, and all divine with Gold.

John Dryden

After the first carefree revelry of the Restoration, King Charles and his ministers were compelled to get down to the practical business of governing the country and repairing the ravages caused by twenty years of war and unstable government. The prospect was daunting.

Two immediate problems presented themselves. One was what was to be done about those who, in rebelling against the crown and participating in an illegal Republican administration, were clearly criminals in the eyes of the old regime now restored. The other was how to compensate the many loyal subjects who had suffered in fortune and estate for their loyalty to the royal cause.

The two questions were obviously closely linked, and were in fact dealt with together. The Act of Indemnity and Oblivion finally became law at the end of August 1660, but in its passage through Parliament, extended throughout the summer, it aroused such protracted argument and such bitter feelings that it frequently seemed that the bill would never be passed. Only the unwearying patience of the King brought eventual agreement, and when the royal assent was finally given the mood of the old Cavaliers was reflected in the contemporary gibe that the Act was one of indemnity for the King's enemies and oblivion for his friends.

It was not in the nature of Charles II to be vindictive; his dearest wish was that his subjects should live together in amity, without undue harping on the passions of the recent past. In this he was in complete accord with his chief adviser, Sir Edward Hyde, and the aims of the Restoration had been laid down in the Declaration of Breda, drawn up by Hyde in the name of the King. As regards indemnity the pertinent passage in that document read as follows:

And to the end that the fear of punishment may not engage any, conscious to themselves of what is passed, to a perseverance in guilt for the future, by opposing the quiet and happiness of their country in the restoration both of king, peers and people to their just, ancient and fundamental rights, we do by these presents declare, that we do grant a free and general pardon, which we are ready upon demand to pass under our Great Seal of England, to all our subjects, of what degree or quality soever, who within forty days after the publishing hereof shall lay hold upon this our grace and favour, and shall by any public act declare their doing so, and that they return to the loyalty and obedience of good subjects (excepting only such persons as shall hereafter be excepted by Parliament). Those only excepted, let all our loving subjects, how faulty soever, rely upon the word of a king, solemnly given by this present Declaration, that no crime whatsoever committed against us or our royal father before the publication of this shall ever rise in judgement or be brought in question against any of them, to the least endamagement of them either in their lives, liberties of their estates, or (as far forth as lies in our power) so much as to the prejudice of their reputations by any reproach or term of distinction from the rest of our best subjects, we desiring and ordaining that henceforward all notes of discord, separation and difference of parties be utterly abolished among all our subjects, whom we invite and conjure to a perfect union among themselves, under our protection, for the resettlement of our just rights and theirs in a free Parliament, by which, upon the word of a king, we will be advised.

Both Charles and Clarendon were anxious that these promises should be fulfilled and be seen to be fulfilled. In accordance with their wishes the Indemnity Bill was introduced in the Commons within a fortnight of the presentation to the House of the Declaration of Breda, and thirteen days before King Charles landed at Dover. It was given its first and second readings on 12 May, and the King may have been optimistic enough to hope that it would be ready for him in its final form when he arrived in London. He was bitterly disappointed.

The trouble lay in that parenthetical clause in the Declaration which referred to pardon being extended to all who returned to their duty 'excepting such persons as shall hereafter be excepted by Parliament'. King Charles had all along made it clear that he would not pardon those who had been directly involved in the murder of his father; that he regarded as a matter of family honour. But so far as the death penalty went he wanted it to stop there; others who submitted could expect clemency in accordance with the terms of the Declaration. But he had expressly granted to Parliament the right to make exceptions. And the Convention Parliament was more fiercely royalist than the King.

The result was that the debates were interminable. Exception after exception to indemnity was urged in the Commons. Many of those involved in government during the interregnum were members of the new Parliament; private enmities were ventilated, and new-found loyalty was not enough to guarantee security. At one point a bold young member declared that 'he that first drew his sword against the King committed as high an offence as he that cut off the King's head,' thus suggesting that any old Republican soldier might be liable to execution. This over-zealous enthusiast was suppressed by the Speaker; but others were almost as venomous. When the King first met his Parliament at Westminster no progress had been made with the bill.

So it went on during June and the first half of July. And the irony of it all was that, while the Commons haggled over who should be excepted from pardon, a majority of the real regicides had managed to escape to the Continent. One man on whom the members were particularly keen to lay hands was the masked executioner who had actually cut off the head of Charles I. His identity, however, was never discovered. Meanwhile the height of absurdity was reached with the proposal that Sir Richard Onslow should be excepted from pardon because, in a wartime speech, he had compared the King with a hedgehog, saying that he had wrapped himself up in his own bristles.

At last, after repeated adjurations from the King, the Commons passed the bill early in July and sent it up to the Lords; twenty names were excepted from the pardon list. But the Lords proved fully as vindictive as the lower house. The majority of peers had been Cavaliers who had suffered exile or persecution under Republican rule, and they were in no mood to show mercy to their former oppressors. They drew up two lists: one of those who had sat in judgement on Charles I, the other of those who had signed the death warrant. It was voted that those named in either should be excepted absolutely from pardon.

The King's patience was sorely tried. On 27 July he went to the House of Lords and delivered a forceful speech. 'When I first came hither to you, which was within two or three days after I came to Whitehall,' he began, 'I did with as much earnestness as I could, both by myself and the Chancellor, recommend to you and the House of Commons the speedy dispatch of the Act of Indemnity as a necessary foundation of that security we all pray for . . . I will not deny it to you, I thought the House of Commons too long about that work; and therefore, now it is come up to you, I would not have you guilty of the same delay.' He thanked God that his intentions and resolutions were the same now as they had been at Breda, and he warned the Lords that 'if you do not join with me in extinguishing this fear which keeps the hearts of men awake and apprehensive of safety and security, you keep me from performing my promise, which if I had not made, I am persuaded neither I nor you had been now here.' He concluded by imploring the House to 'depart from all particular animosities and revenge, or memory of past provocations', and to pass the bill 'without other exceptions than of those who were immediately guilty of that murder of my father'.

There were still further arguments, and towards the end of August the Lords sent the bill back to the Commons with their amendments. At last a compromise was reached, and the bill received the royal assent on 29 August. In its final form it offered a general pardon for past treasons; excluded by name were thirty regicides, while six others were excepted as regards punishment other than death.

Then came the trials, the result of which was of course a foregone conclusion. Each rebel received the usual sentence for high treason; he was to be drawn on a hurdle to the place of execution, hanged, cut down alive, castrated, disembowelled and quartered. And in this case the popular clamour for vengeance demanded all the rigour of the law.

The executions began in October at Charing Cross, where the maximum number of spectators could be accommodated; the first to die was the regicide Thomas Harrison, who met his end with conspicuous courage. So did most of the others. But when ten men had died the King called a halt. The rest of the sentences were suspended until he, by the advice of Parliament, should decide whether they were to be carried out.

It was not quite the end of the matter. Three more regicides, captured from Holland, were hanged in the following year, and a new bill was proposed in the Commons for the execution of those reprieved. The matter was disposed of in council notes between Charles and Hyde. 'What is to be wished should be done,' minuted the Chancellor, 'in the Bill that is now ordered to be brought in for the execution of those ill men who are condemned? Would it not be better that the Bill should sleep in the Houses, and not be brought to you?' Charles replied: 'I must confess that I am weary of hanging except upon new offences.' The bill was allowed to drop.

In the case of one man King Charles, for political reasons, fell short of his usual standard of clemency. The fiery revolutionary Sir Henry Vane, though excepted from full pardon by the Convention Parliament, had not been an actual regicide. He was brought to trial in June 1662 on a charge of high treason, and was condemned to death after making a spirited defence. He gloried in his republicanism and would clearly be a menace to the throne if allowed to go free. King Charles wrote to the Chancellor:

> The relation that has been made to me of Sir H. Vane's carriage yesterday in the Hall is the occasion of this letter, which, if I am rightly informed, was so insolent as to justify all he had done, acknowledging no supreme power in England but a Parliament, and many things to that purpose. You have had a true account of all, and, if he has new occasion to be hanged, certainly he is too dangerous a man to let live, if we can honestly put him out of the way.

Vane was allowed to die, the pretext being that his republican activities constituted new offences. But in his case the King commuted the sentence of hanging, drawing and quartering to beheading.

The vengeance taken on the rebels seems in retrospect a bloodthirsty business. So, of course, it was; but not excessively so according to the ideas of the seventeenth century. And some severity was necessary in order to secure the stability of the restored regime. Republican and seditious ideas had not been stamped out, as was shown by Venner's rising early in 1661; and indeed there was always a danger of a new revolution during the reign of Charles II. But the executions

7*

of 1660 showed the populace that disaffection would be met with firm action.

A more serious question in the long term, though it did not impress itself so spectacularly on the public eye, was that of land settlement. All through the reign the government of Charles II suffered from financial embarrassment. This was nothing unusual; most governments at all times are short of money, and in England since the end of the Middle Ages only Henry VII and Elizabeth I had achieved much success in keeping the crown solvent. But Charles II encountered exceptional difficulties. Civil war, Cromwell's naval campaigns, and the innumerable problems of keeping an illegal administration in power, culminating in the near-anarchy of 1659–60, had had their inevitable effect; it was no fault of King Charles that he inherited a bankrupt treasury. And when he and his advisers were at their wits' end to raise revenue and restore the shattered finances of a devastated country they were at the same time expected, not unreasonably, to compensate innumerable loyalists for the sacrifices they had made in keeping the King's cause alive.

The problem was in fact insoluble. Many of the old Cavaliers were ruined, their land confiscated, their incomes reduced to nothing by fines and sequestrations. They naturally hoped that the King for whom they had struggled and fought would restore them to their former affluence. But this the King was utterly unable to do. He had not the money to compensate them financially; and as for the estates, the position was inextricably confused. Much of the property, seized from the Cavalier owners and used to reward the followers of Cromwell and the Republicans, had since changed hands many times. It would have been quite impracticable to evict all the existing holders from land which they had acquired in good faith; to attempt to do so would have been to invite a new revolution. General Monk in particular, whose prestige as the saviour of the monarchy gave him an authority enjoyed by no other subject, insisted that those of his soldiers who had bought up confiscated land should not be deprived of it, and it was his urging especially that compelled King Charles's government to confirm the sale of confiscated land.

There was really no other possible course. All that Charles could do for his loyal followers was to see that those who had rendered him personal service did not go unrewarded. The gallant Jane Lane, who had helped him so nobly in his flight after Worcester, received a variety of costly presents; the Penderel brothers, who had befriended him in the same episode, were given pensions; Captain Tattersall, in whose ship he had sailed to safety in France, was put in command of a naval vessel; and others were similarly honoured. It was little enough, but it helped to salve the royal conscience.

For the Cavaliers in general nothing could be done, and clauses in the Act of Indemnity and Oblivion, while hedged about with exceptions, laid down the principle that those now in possession of land that had changed hands since 1642 were not to be disturbed. That this was grossly unfair to the old Cavaliers was not to be doubted, and its effect on the future course of the reign was profound, though to what extent is difficult to estimate. A manifest injustice at the outset of the Restoration gave rise to a rankling sense of grievance among the most ardent supporters of the Stewart monarchy, and the change that came over the Cavalier Parliament, so strongly royalist in its early days, can be attributed at least in part to the resentment felt by the old landed families.

This Parliament met in May 1661, a fortnight after King Charles's coronation. The Convention had done its work in confirming the return of monarchy and in laying down the general lines of the Restoration settlement, and it was dissolved on Christmas Eve, 1660. Elections were held in the spring of the following year, and the new House of Commons, as was inevitable in the general climate of opinion, consisted mainly of Cavalier squires ready to do all the King should ask them to do. The Parliament was destined to last, through many vicissitudes, until 1679, its life of eighteen years being only two years short of the twenty achieved by the Long Parliament, the longest in English history; but that historic assembly, with all its ups and downs, purges and expulsions, cannot really be said to have had a continuous existence. The Cavalier Parliament, long before its long life was over, was to prove itself a source of formidable opposition to the sovereign in whose name it sat.

But this was in the future. The early 1660s were a time of at least outward prosperity and general rejoicing. The King's popularity was undimmed. His easy manners and genial accessibility appealed to high and low; possibly no monarch in English history (certainly none since Elizabeth) had enjoyed such general appeal, and the people took him to their hearts.

Nothing was allowed to interfere with this popularity. There was indeed a royal scandal towards the end of 1660, when it was revealed that the Duke of York had been secretly married to Anne Hyde, the Chancellor's daughter; but this affair, though it aroused something approaching hysteria in Hyde himself and fury in some members of the royal family, caused little perturbation outside the inner circles of the court. The good sense with which Charles handled it saw to that.

The other untoward event, the rising of Venner and his Fifth Monarchy fanatics, was again little more than a nine days' wonder. A fair amount of blood was shed, but the outbreak was soon suppressed, though the memory of it caused prolonged uneasiness.

Charles II was crowned in Westminster Abbey on St George's Day 1661. It was his second coronation, as he had been through that dour Presbyterian ceremony at Scone just ten years before, celebrated rather with lengthy sermons than with pageantry. The English coronation was an altogether more splendid affair.

Before it the King created sixty-eight Knights of the Bath and a number of peers. It was on this occasion that Lord Hyde (he had been raised to the peerage in November 1660) was given the Earldom of Clarendon, and another individual

honoured soon after for services to the crown was Roger
Palmer, who became Earl of Castlemaine; the wife whom he
had so kindly lent to his sovereign thus became a countess,
and although she was not yet a peeress in her own right, the
succession to the title was limited to the heirs of *her* body, not
that of her husband: 'the reason whereof,' Pepys commented,
'everybody knows.'

Early on 22 April Charles went by barge to the Tower of
London, traditional starting-point of the coronation ceremonies,
and from there rode in state back to Whitehall. 'The King,
in a most rich imbrodered suit and cloak, looked most nobly.'
Such was the comment of Pepys, eager as always to see everything that was going on. On the following day the busy young
civil servant was even more in evidence, managing to squeeze
himself not only into the Abbey but later into Westminster
Hall where the Coronation Banquet was held.

The coronation itself aroused the greatest enthusiasm. The
ancient ritual symbolized the return to the ancient order of
things after the rigours of revolutionary Puritanism. The old
regalia had been sold or destroyed during the interregnum,
but had been replaced immediately after the Restoration.
Charles himself played his part to perfection. It was a glorious
April day, and he was cheered to the echo when he rode,
robed and bare-headed, from Whitehall Palace to Westminster
Hall and then proceeded on foot to the Abbey. Pepys to his
great regret could not see the central ceremony from where he
was, but he heard the 'great shout' that arose when the crown
was put on the royal head. 'And he came forth to the Throne
and there passed more ceremonies: as, taking the oath and
having things read to him by the Bishopp, and his lords (who
put on their capps as soon as the King put on his Crowne)
and Bishopps came and kneeled before him.' 'The Bishopp'
alluded to by Pepys was Gilbert Sheldon, Bishop of London,
who performed most of the duties of the Primate on behalf of
the ailing Juxon.

The banquet followed, and Pepys saw the King's Champion,

'all in armor on horseback, with his speare and targett carried before him', fling down his gauntlet in challenge to any who might dispute the King's right to his title. 'At last, when he is come, the King Drinkes to him and then sends him the Cup, which is of gold; and he drinks it off and then rides back again with the cup in his hand.'

It was a glorious day, and Pepys finished it appropriately by getting thoroughly drunk; roaming through streets, kissing any women friends he met, drinking the loyal toast on his knees, and wondering 'to see how the ladies did tipple'. At last he found himself in the house of Mr Thornbury the yeoman of the King's wine cellar; 'and there, with his wife and two sisters and some gallant sparks that were there, we drank the King's health and nothing else, till one of the genlemen fell down stark drunk and there lay speweing.' Before the night was out Pepys had himself done his own share of spewing.

The next important event was the King's marriage. Charles was anxious to marry a European princess and father a family of royal children to make the succession secure: a thing that in the event he never succeeded in doing. There were several possible candidates, but some were ruled out by the King's personal predilections. He was opposed to a French alliance because of the resentment he felt against his treatment by Cardinal Mazarin, and he had little love for Germans. 'Odd's fish, they are all foggy,' he is said to have remarked on the charms of German ladies. There was no Spanish bride available, and at length the choice fell on the Portuguese Princess Catherine of Braganza. She brought the territories of Bombay and Tangier as dowry to the English crown.

On the whole the alliance was reasonably popular in England. A Protestant princess would have been preferred, but with the elimination of Germans it was difficult to find one. Portugal was favoured as England's oldest ally, and the Princess herself was a simple, good-natured, innocent, unobtrusive girl, nine years younger than the King, to whom it was impossible to object on personal grounds. The people, moreover, were ready

to agree at this time to almost anything the King chose to do,
and when the news of the betrothal came through there was
plenty of enthusiasm. On 27 June 1662 Pepys recorded a
singularly unseemly, if intensely loyal, form of royal toast in
honour of the happy pair.

When Catherine arrived, on 14 May 1662, King Charles's
impression was one of modified rapture. He wrote diplomatically
to the Queen of Portugal:

> Being now freed from dread of the sea and enjoying in this
> springtime the company of my dearest wife, I am the happiest
> man in the world and the most enamoured, seeing close at
> hand the loveliness of her person and her virtues, not only
> those which Your Majesty mentioned in your letter—
> simplicity, gentleness and prudence—but many others also . . .
> May the good God preserve her to me and grant Your
> Majesty long years of life, in which to be a comfort to us
> both.

His summing-up to Clarendon was not quite so ardent.

> It was happy for the honour of the nation, [he wrote on
> the morning after he had received his bride at Portsmouth]
> that I was not put to the consummation of the marriage last
> night; for I was so sleepy by having slept but two hours
> in my journey as I was afraid that matters would have gone
> very sleepily. I can only now give you an account of what
> I have seen a-bed; which, in short, is, her face is not so
> exact as to be called a beauty, though her eyes are excellent
> good, and not anything in her face that in the least degree
> can shock one. On the contrary, she has as much agreeable-
> ness in her looks altogether, as ever I saw: and if I have any
> skill in physiognomy, which I think I have, she must be
> as good a woman as ever was born.

The marriage was not an unhappy one. Charles made no

pretence of marital fidelity, but this was perfectly normal in royal alliances. Catherine, young and innocent, at first resented this; but as she grew more mature she accepted the position gracefully and became the model of a gracious and dignified consort. In the early days of marriage also there was a conflict curiously reminiscent of the union of King Charles's father with Henrietta Maria. On arrival in England at the age of fifteen, Henrietta had brought with her a train of French attendants whose intrigues for a time bade fair to wreck the marriage. When Charles I at length put his foot down and dispatched them back to France there were at first scenes and tantrums; but it was after this that King Charles fell deeply and lastingly in love with his young wife.

Similarly Catherine was accompanied to England by a number of pious and forbidding Portuguese ladies and some gloomy clerics. King Charles could not stand their presence, and when he expressed his determination to send them packing there was similar resentment from the young Queen. When this had blown over, the King fed his wife's natural jealousies by insisting on making the Countess of Castlemaine one of the Ladies of the Queen's Bedchamber. It was a needless insult and humiliation for Queen Catherine, and this was the one great quarrel of their married life.

Eventually, however, they settled down, and though, in contrast with the last generation, there was never any question of a love match, the oddly assorted couple lived their lives in mutual affection and respect. Catherine presided over the court with grace and gave unstinting support to her husband. He for his part treated her with unwavering consideration, and when, in the anti-popery hysteria that developed in the latter part of the reign, she was attacked as a papist, he guarded and defended her with the fiercest loyalty.

Catherine's prime duty was of course to provide an heir to the throne, and here she failed. From time to time there were rumours of a royal pregnancy, but as the years rolled on it became obvious that the marriage was destined to be unfruitful. The Queen herself was desperately anxious. In October 1663 she had a serious illness, and in her delirium dreamed that she had produced a multiple birth. King Charles nursed her with devoted care, giving the lie to those who maintained that he wanted to be rid of her and find some more fecund wife; but from this time he accepted the fact that, so long as the marriage lasted, he would have no legitimate issue and that the Duke of York would remain the heir to the throne.

The barrenness of the marriage was no fault of the King's. As early as 1649 he had fathered a son by Lucy Walter, and in the years that followed there were children by Barbara Palmer, Louise de Kéroualle, Nell Gwyn and many other ladies, most of them openly acknowledged and some of them raised to the peerage. He was indeed a prolific father, the number of whose offspring has never been even roughly estimated. And he tried his best with the Queen; the failure distressed both of them.

For the rest, King Charles was a happy man in those early years of the Restoration. There were storm-clouds on the horizon, mostly financial and religious; but he did not let them worry him. Public affairs were capably handled by the Earl of Clarendon, and though Charles was never a political cipher he had implicit trust in his chief minister and made no attempt to take things into his own hands. He was content to preside over the social life of the country, showing himself to his people and basking in his popularity. His life was one of constant activity; he played tennis at Whitehall and Hampton Court, attended the races at Newmarket, swam in the Thames, and increased the number of his mistresses. Lady Castlemaine was still the reigning favourite, but she had her rivals, the most notable being the lovely but reputedly empty-headed Frances Stewart. She was possibly not so stupid as she was made out to be, and it may have been through motives of cold policy that she so resolutely refused to share the royal bed; she finally braved her sovereign's wrath by marrying the Duke of Richmond.

Foreign policy in these years was complicated, and diplomatic activity tortuous; but there was little to trouble the heads
of the British people. At the time of the Restoration England
was technically at war with Spain, but there was no fighting
in progress and a peace was quickly negotiated to the satisfaction of both countries. From that time on, however, Britain
tended more towards friendship with France, a policy which
accorded with King Charles's own inclinations. In 1662 he
came to an agreement whereby Dunkirk, the last British
possession on the mainland of Europe, was transferred to
France for a sum of £400,000. The transfer was unpopular
in England, but the garrison had cost more than £100,000 a
year to keep up, and money was scarce.

For all the minor troubles that afflicted the state, and the
Government's perennial difficulty in raising money to keep
the administration going, the first five years of the restored
regime were a time of peace, reasonable prosperity and general
happiness. Charles and Clarendon ruled the country with skill
and sureness of touch, and the people basked in the euphoria
induced by the Restoration. But in 1665 there came a change.

In the first place England went to war. From almost the
beginning of the century there had been intense rivalry,
principally at sea, between the English and the Dutch. There
had been constant friction over the herring fisheries in the
North Sea and over the wool trade. Involved with this was
the British claim to sovereignty over the Narrow Seas round
the south and east coasts of England, a claim resented and
challenged by the Netherlands. In 1652 the First Dutch War
had broken out; it lasted for some two years and was chiefly
remarkable for the high seamanship shown by the rival admirals
Robert Blake and Marten van Tromp, the two finest sailors
of the day. Blake had had the last word, and the Dutch were
still smarting for revenge.

A number of incidents at sea during the first years of the
Restoration led up to renewal of hostilities. In these the British
were more often than not the aggressors; there was a strong

war party in England, led by the Duke of York, anxious to goad the Dutch into action. Their inclinations were strengthened by King Charles's deliberately pro-French policy, for the Dutch were the implacable enemies of the monarchy of Louis XIV. This combination of circumstances made a renewed struggle inevitable, and the Dutch declared war on 14 January 1665.

The Second Dutch War, fought almost entirely at sea, was, like so many of its kind at that period, indecisive in its results. As has been said, the nature of seventeenth-century naval warfare, involving up to a hundred small vessels on each side, hard for a commander to control and subject to the vagaries of wind and weather, made outright victory a rare occurrence. The English navy held its own until 1667, though it could boast no admiral equal to Michael de Ruyter. The war, however, meant a terrible strain on the meagre resources of the English crown. It was financial stringency rather than any naval incapacity that led to the final humiliation of June 1667 when, the fleet having been laid up, the Dutch sailed unopposed up the Medway, burned four warships and towed away the *Royal Charles*, Britain's largest vessel and the pride of the fleet.

The Medway disaster was a moral rather than a material defeat for England. The peace that was soon afterwards patched up was a truce in which neither country gained any significant advantage, and Anglo-Dutch hostilities were renewed some five years later. But the effects of the event on internal English politics were far-reaching.

The hostilities themselves, however, made little impact on the lives of Englishmen. War in the seventeenth century was a matter for professionals, if we may include in their ranks the unfortunate individuals drawn into the fight by way of the press-gang. The Second Dutch War, whatever its problems for the government and its effect on the future monarchy, meant little to the nation at large. The people of England, and of its capital city in particular, were far more concerned with matters unconnected with war or high policy. For during the course of hostilities occurred the two great internal disasters of Charles II's reign.

There was severe frost in the early months of 1665. It broke in March, being followed by a season of drought: 'the driest that ever man knew,' according to Richard Baxter, 'or our forefathers mention of late ages; so that the grounds were burnt like the highways where the cattle should have fed.' The drought lasted till September, with a brief interval of rain in August; and it was in this parched atmosphere that the Great Plague broke out.

In the crowded and insanitary city that was seventeenth-century London plague in one form or another was endemic. There had been terrible outbreaks in 1603 and 1625, the two years in which one sovereign had died and another succeeded though there is no need to attach any significance to the coincidence. In the unsettled years 1640–1647 pestilence had raged almost incessantly. Earlier, in the fifteenth and sixteenth centuries, there had been frequent major outbreaks, and back in the Middle Ages there had been the worst calamity of all, the Black Death of the mid-fourteenth century, which had devastated the whole of Europe and most of the known world. Every year in London there were a certain number of deaths attributed to 'plague'. But since 1647 there had been no widespread infection. The pestilence of 1625 was still known as 'the Great Plague', the worst outbreak since the Middle Ages.

That title it now lost. The plague of 1665 so eclipsed the memory of previous outbreaks that they have been consigned to the limbo of history. They are hardly mentioned in modern chronicles of their times (apart of course from the Black Death); the Great Plague of 1665 reigns in sombre majesty as the supreme natural disaster of modern British history. Before it was brought under control it caused the deaths of more than 100,000 people in London alone. The official death-roll for 1625 had been 41,313, and for 1603 33,347.

It is impossible to say just when the epidemic of 1665

started, for the first deaths were accepted as normal and excited little attention. There were, however, portents from the heavens that, as the pestilence raged, assumed tremendous significance in the minds of men. A comet was seen at Christmas 1664, and a second blazed across the sky in the following March. It was somewhere about this time that the mortality began to be noticed, and from then on other signs of the wrath of God were reported as having been seen. Astrologers were busy, and broadsheets such as William Lilly's Almanack, predicting death and destruction at the dictates of the stars, passed from hand to hand.

The place of origin can be stated with a little more certainty. It was not in the city proper but in what were then the suburbs that the plague first made itself felt. Deaths were reported in Drury Lane and in the parish of St Giles in the Fields, where Tottenham Court Road now meets Oxford Street, and thence the infection spread rapidly eastwards once the hot weather began. Samuel Pepys, here as always the prime authority on what was going on in London, recorded on 30 April: 'Great fears of the Sickenesse here in the City, it being said that two or three houses are already shut up. God preserve us all.'

Symptoms of the malady were unpleasant and painful—high fever with swelling of the lymphatic glands, spots on the skin, bleeding from the nose or mouth, stomach disorders, feelings of suffocation in the throat and chest, ending in coma or delirium. The swellings, or 'buboes', drove people mad with pain, and some ran naked into the streets, foaming at the mouth and shrieking in agony. Medical historians are agreed on the diagnosis of bubonic plague, caused by a bacillus carried by rat fleas. There was no known cure.

As the pestilence increased, the authorities—the Lord Mayor and aldermen in the City, magistrates in the suburbs—took what measures they could. Plague nurses were sent into the houses; they were mostly dirty and drunken hags who alone could be persuaded for the meagre pay to undertake the dangerous and unsavoury work, and who mercilessly robbed the dead and the dying. Attempts to cut off the infection were made; whole households were isolated, and dwellings shut up with the victims inside, the doors marked with a large red cross. Pepys saw this sign for the first time on 7 June:

> This day, much against my Will, I did in Drury-lane see two or three houses marked with a red cross upon the doors, and 'Lord have mercy upon us' writ there—which was a sad sight to me, being the first of that kind that to my remembrance I ever saw. It put me into an ill conception of myself and my smell, so that I was forced to buy some roll-tobacco to smell to and chaw—which took away the apprehension.

As the months passed, and the epidemic swelled to terrifying dimensions, the atmosphere of London, never salubrious, became almost unbearable. Huge plague pits were dug for burial, but rotting corpses still lay in many streets, and the stench can be imagined. The symptoms seemed to become more virulent as time went on; victims who ventured to stir beyond their doors sometimes dropped dead in the open air, and their bodies lay where they died until the inadequate corps of labourers raised for the purpose could drag them to the nearest plague pit.

Normal life in the City was at a standstill. Shops, taverns and theatres were closed; all sport was forbidden, and residents were ordered to be within their doors by nine o'clock in the evening. Naturally everybody who could get away escaped from the stricken city. All who had means to do so bolted into the country, many of them taking with them the seeds of the dread disease, to start new if lesser outbreaks in hitherto healthy areas. The roads were filled with coaches and wagons taking refugees and their worldly goods away from London.

Thus it was that by midsummer only the poorer classes and those whose livelihood made flight impossible remained in the metropolis. The richer sort had put as much space as they could between themselves and the capital. The courtiers of Whitehall

were anxious to get away, but the King showed no undue
haste. It would have been folly to risk the lives of the royal
family and all members of the government, and nobody would
have blamed him if he had departed earlier than he did; but
he was anxious to keep the wheels of administration turning.
It was not till 9 July that King Charles, with the Duke of York
and Prince Rupert, moved up-river to Hampton Court. At the
beginning of August King, court and Privy Council made a
further move to Salisbury, and in September to Oxford.

A few men in the higher ranks of life stayed in London.
Foremost among them was George Monk Duke of Albemarle,
the man who above all others had guided the Restoration to
its triumphant climax. He now took up residence at the Cockpit
in St James's, and as the one remaining representative of the
central government co-ordinated the work of local authorities
and prevented all law and order from breaking down. His most
active lieutenant was William Earl of Craven, a man of great
wealth and conspicuous gallantry; he kept his house in Drury
Lane open for the sick and distressed, whose very presence
was a danger to himself, and distributed money to supply the
necessities of the poor and destitute. Others who stayed at
their posts and did valuable work in the emergency were the
Archbishop of Canterbury, Gilbert Sheldon, and Lord Brouncker,
a Commissioner of the Navy. The Lord Mayor of London,
Sir William Lawrence, showed constant courage in the most
difficult and dangerous circumstances.

The pestilence reached new heights at the end of August.
In the last week of the month more than 6,000 were admitted
to have died in London of plague, nearly 2,000 more than in
the week before. In reality the figure must have been higher,
for parish authorities tended to minimize their own casualties
and deaths were put down to other causes if the slightest
excuse could be found. In September came rain and cooler
weather, but at first this had no effect on the spread of infection.
The plague pits were full, and there was no wood left for
coffins. More and more corpses lay rotting in the streets.

The worst week of all was actually in mid-September. From the 12th to the 19th of the month, out of a total of 8,297 deaths in London, 7,165 were recorded as being due to plague. Again the real toll was probably considerably higher. Pepys, who had moved to Woolwich where he was carrying on his navy duties, heard the figures from the Duke of Albemarle when he went to him to report on the state of the fleet.

> But Lord, what a sad time it is, [he confided to his diary] to see no boats upon the River—and grass grow all up and down Whitehall-court—and nobody but poor wretches in the streets. And which is worst of all, the Duke showed us the number of the plague this week, brought in the last night from the Lord Mayor—that it is encreased about 600 more than the last, which is quite contrary to all our hopes and expectations from the coldness of the late season.

In fact, however, the worst was over. From the latter part of September onwards the mortality gradually decreased, and by the end of November the figures had fallen to some 400 a week. But in the meantime the plague had been spreading throughout England. Refugees from London had a miserable time. No town would admit them if it could help it, and thousands had to find what shelter they could in the open fields; many of them starved to death or died from exposure. The harshest measures enforced by local authorities were mostly in vain. Nothing could keep the pestilence within bounds. Nowhere was there anything like the havoc experienced in London, but most of the larger towns of England were affected in greater or lesser degree. Southampton suffered particularly badly, as did Dover; congested dockside areas were fertile breeding-grounds for plague. Moving northwards, the disease struck Leicester, Ipswich and Yarmouth, and stretched as far as the Tyne. Westwards, Bristol and Gloucester suffered severely.

One remote village, Eyam in Derbyshire, achieved lasting

fame for its tragic heroism. It boasted some 350 inhabitants, most of whom had hardly heard of London. But in September 1665 a box of clothing arrived from the capital for the local tailor. A fortnight later the tailor was dead and sickness was spreading through the village. In the cold winter months it subsided, but in the spring of 1666, when London and the larger towns were returning to normal, it struck again with terrible force. Those who could get away in the early stages did so, but in July, when the number of dead began to exceed the living, a grim decision was taken.

The rector of Eyam was a young man of twenty-seven, the Rev. William Mompesson. He it was who took command of the situation, telling his handful of parishioners that it was their duty as Christians to stay where they were and not let the plague spread further. They accepted his decision. A boundary line was drawn around the village, and it was vowed that nobody would go beyond it.

It is said that only one villager broke the vow—a woman whose family had all died. She made for the town of Tideswell five miles away, but was detected and driven back. The rest faced death in their homes.

Mompesson worked incessantly for his flock. He held services in the open air, and preached sermons exhorting the people to remain steadfast and keep the pestilence within the village. When in October the plague suddenly ceased, there were fewer than forty villagers left alive. Remarkably, Mompesson was one of them; but his wife was among the victims.

In London the Plague lingered on, though greatly diminished. Nearly 2,000 deaths were recorded between January and September 1666. Then the remnants of the disease were obliterated in the most drastic manner possible.

On Sunday, 2 September 1666, Samuel Pepys, who was living in Seething Lane, recorded:

Some of our maids sitting up late last night to get things ready for our feast today, Jane called us, about 3 in the morning, to tell us of a great fire they saw in the City. So I rose, and slipped on my nightgown and went to her window, and I thought it to be on the back side of Markelane at the furthest.

This was the beginning of the Great Fire of London, the most famous conflagration in the history of the capital. It was by no means the first of its kind, and was perhaps not even the greatest. Far back in the reign of King Edgar the whole city had been destroyed, and this outbreak was followed in the early Middle Ages by a series of serious fires. In that of 1212 3,000 people were said to have perished: a remarkable contrast with that of 1666, in which the death-roll, considering the extent of the material damage, was minimal. But of these earlier disasters nothing is known beyond the bare facts as mentioned in the chronicles. The Great Fire of Charles II's reign is fully documented.

Pepys, not regarding what he saw from Jane's window as anything much out of the ordinary, went back to bed. At seven he rose and 'saw the fire not so much as it was, and further off'. But a little later Jane came to him with more news; she had heard that more than 300 houses had been destroyed during the night and that the fire 'was now burning down all Fishstreet by London Bridge'. Evidently this was no ordinary blaze, and Pepys, eager as always to see all that was going on, dressed and hurried off to the Tower, where he 'got up upon one of the high places' and viewed the devastation below. The fire was raging furiously; houses and churches were ablaze, and the riverside was thronged with people loading their belongings into boats or flinging them into the water in the hope of retrieving them later.

The fire had started at one o'clock in the morning in the house of Thomas Farriner, the King's baker, in Pudding Lane (it did not, as the story was put about later, end at Pye Corner). Farriner had left his oven inadequately extinguished, and he awoke to find his house on fire. He escaped with his household except for one maidservant who was trapped in the flames and died; she was the first of the few human victims of the Great Fire.

The summer had been a dry one, and with the wind blowing from the east the flames spread, with terrifying but hardly surprising rapidity, in a great arc northward and westward. By mid-morning they were quite out of control. Such fire-fighting appliances as existed were hopelessly inadequate, and the same might be said of the chief official of the City of London. Sir William Lawrence, the Lord Mayor who had stuck to his post with such gallantry during the Great Plague, had been succeeded by Sir Thomas Bludworth, who proved himself sadly ineffective in this second disaster. He was called from his bed in his house near Aldersgate at about three a.m. when the watchmen and constables found themselves unable to deal with the flames. He dressed and went to the scene but was resentful at being disturbed; and he expressed his resentment in words that were held against him for many a year. 'Pish!' he said, 'a woman might piss it out.'

Bludworth's first impression should perhaps not be held too strongly against him; it was much the same as that of Pepys, though the difference was that his was the position of responsibility. But in the hours that followed he was equally ineffectual. Having delivered his verdict he returned to bed, but was soon hauled back again. The fire-fighters wanted his authority to pull down houses in the path of the flames as the only means of stopping the fire; but the proposal was too much for the timid Bludworth. 'Who shall pay the charge of rebuilding the houses?' he asked, and added that he dared not allow them to be destroyed without the consent of the owners. In the vacuum created by the Lord Mayor's abdication of his responsibilities, Pepys himself took action. He held no official position in the City but took it upon himself to appeal to higher authority. He hastened by river to Whitehall, where he gained access to the King.

Little news of the calamity seems up to this time to have

penetrated to the court; but once informed of its gravity King
Charles and his brother assumed control.

> They seemed much troubled, [recorded Pepys] and the
> King commanded me to go to my Lord Mayor from him and
> command him to spare no houses but to pull down before
> the fire every way. The Duke of York bid me tell him that
> if he would have any more soldiers, he shall; and so did my
> Lord Arlington afterward, as a great secret. Here meeting
> with Captain Cocke, I in his coach, which he lent me, and
> Creed with me, to Pauls; and there walked along Watling-
> street as well as I could, every creature coming away loaden
> with goods to save—and here and there sick people carried
> away in beds. Extraordinary goods carried in carts and on
> backs. At last met my Lord Mayor in Canning Streete,
> like a man spent, with a hankercher about his neck. To the
> King's message, he cried like a fainting woman, 'Lord,
> what can I do? I am spent. People will not obey me. I have
> been pulling down houses. But the fire overtakes us faster
> than we can do it.' That he needed no more soldiers; and
> that for himself he must go and refresh himself, having
> been up all night.

Thereafter Sir Thomas Bludworth gave up the struggle.

Meanwhile the King surveyed the scene and took his
measures. He went down the river in his barge and summed up
the situation. Nothing could be hoped for from the City
authorities; nor could the flames be extinguished. All that
could be done was to hold them in check as far as possible and
reduce the panic. The King gave orders for the ruthless pulling
down and blowing up of houses; he called out the trained bands
to restore order and put the Duke of York in charge of fire-
fighting operations.

All through the next day the flames continued to spread, in
spite of the untiring efforts of the Duke and his troops. On
Tuesday the King himself took a hand. Never in all his reign

did he show himself to better advantage. All that day he was to be seen riding through London with grimy face and mud-stained clothes, encouraging the fire-fighters and rewarding good work with guineas; sometimes leaping from his horse to wield axe or fire-bucket himself where the flames were fiercest.

As for the Duke of York, both this day and the next he worked from five a.m. to midnight, directing operations, checking disorder, subduing the panic and taking hardly any rest until at last, on the evening of Wednesday, 5 September, the fire was seen to be under control. Next day, apart from isolated areas where smouldering continued, the worst was over. 'All that is left,' wrote a contemporary, 'both of the City and suburbs, is acknowledged, under God, to be wholly due to the King and the Duke of York.'

There was indeed little left. The fire was checked just beyond the Temple. London Bridge was saved, and a few of the large buildings such as Gresham House in Bishopsgate Street. The Cheshire Cheese, just off Fleet Street, survived to become what it is today, a prime tourist attraction as an example of a seventeenth-century London inn. But only one-sixth of London within the Wall was left standing. Nearly all the city companies' halls had been destroyed, and most of the churches. Above all, St Paul's, London's most towering monument, was just a shell. The great church had in truth become easy fuel for fire. It had been dreadfully neglected, and the fabric had become not only insecure but dangerous. The walls were unsteady, stones were mouldering, and the tower was leaning. A commission headed by Christopher Wren had in fact just been inspecting the Cathedral with a view to restoration, and were arranging for plans and estimates to be prepared. The Great Fire put an end to their work, and what remained of the rotten hulk had to be demolished. But a wealth of history perished with its destruction.

Arrangements were immediately set on foot for rebuilding London. Three plans were submitted—by Christopher Wren, John Evelyn and Robert Hooke. Hooke, Reader of Mathematics

Gresham College, wanted a city built on strictly geometrical principles, with streets running east to westward, north to south in straight lines, parallel with, and at right-angles to, each other. Evelyn, the cosmopolitan scholar, proposed a London continental in style, with open piazzas and a long quay to make a stately river front.

The most grandiose scheme, and the most imaginative, was Wren's. The great architect brought forward a plan which would, without doubt, have made London the most beautiful city in Europe. It combined what was best in Evelyn's and Hooke's ideas, though he worked quite independently and his was in fact the first plan to be completed; almost incredibly, it was submitted to the King and Council on 10 September. His design was for an open city of piazzas, colonnades and fountains, with broad tree-lined thoroughfares running down to the river, vistas in all directions, a majestic St Paul's dominating the skyline, and a stately triumphal arch standing at Ludgate to proclaim the glory of King Charles II.

In the event none of these plans was adopted. From the purely aesthetic point of view this was sad, and connoisseurs of architecture and town-planning have lamented ever since that Wren was not allowed to build a new London of unsurpassed magnificence. But in truth it could not be done. Wren's design was a glorious dream; it would have cost an enormous sum of money which, after the losses of the fire, was simply not available. Moreover the rebuilding on new foundations would have taken an inordinate amount of time. The City's business, interrupted as it was, had to be got going again as quickly as possible if London was to retain its pride of place as a commercial centre.

The objections to Wren's plan applied, if in lesser degree, to Evelyn's and Hooke's as well. So the mundane but practical decision was taken to encourage London's merchants to rebuild immediately on the old sites. Nor was this really a matter for regret if it may be granted that beauty was not the only factor involved. Wren's plan would have wiped away all memory

of the old London which, insanitary as it may have been, was
redolent of centuries of tradition, bound up with the history
of the English people and their capital.

The new London that arose, moreover, was an altogether
finer city than the one that had been destroyed. The old wooden
hovels that had been so susceptible to plague and fire had been
swept away and were not to be restored. A royal proclamation
issued immediately after the fire ordained that:

> the woeful experience in this late visitation hath sufficiently
> convinced all men of the pernicious consequences which
> have attended the building with timber, and even with
> stone itself, and the notable benefit of brick, which in so
> many places hath resisted and even extinguished the Fire:
> and we do hereby declare our express will and pleasure,
> that no man whatsoever shall presume to erect any house
> or building, great or small, but of brick or stone; and if
> any man shall do the contrary, the next magistrate shall
> forthwith cause it to be pulled down, and such farther course
> shall be taken for his punishment as he deserves.

And so, in the months and years that followed, the City of
London as we know it today came into being—a city of brick
and stone, of splendid buildings and majestic churches, on the
lines of the old streets whose names proclaimed the heritage of
centuries. Since the rebuilding there has been no outbreak of
plague in London, and no fire comparable with the disaster
of 1666.

Christopher Wren busied himself with designing a new
St Paul's Cathedral, new churches, and replacements for some
of the greater buildings. In the restoration of the City of London
in general the driving force was the personal influence of King
Charles. Walter G. Bell, still the prime authority on the subject,
wrote:

> It is my belief that London as it was re-created after the Fire

owed more (always apart from Wren's individual buildings, which glorified it) to King Charles II than to Sir Christopher Wren. His was the active, agitating mind. His hand was seen everywhere. So soon as the ruins were cold, he appointed a committee of Lords of the Council, the Lord Chancellor being at its head, to consult with the City's representative upon the rebuilding. After the Act of Parliament had passed, he desired the Lord Mayor and Aldermen, by mediation and advice, to have things done as should contribute 'to the beauty, ornament, and convenience of the City,' even beyond the authority given them by the strict letter of the statute, promising therein all assistance in his Royal power. His concern for the grandeur of the principal streets led him to recommend that where end buildings of cross streets abutted on high streets, they should range in height and façade with those of the high streets. The King proposed that the Halls of the lesser Companies be erected next to the Thames Quay, adding thereby to the beauty of the river frontage. He wished sufficient market space to be provided to make unnecessary any markets in the open streets.

The bright dawn of the Restoration faded with the troubles of 1665–67. War and natural calamities combined to bring about a new era. The humiliation of the Medway incursion led to the fall of Clarendon, the coming to power of a clique of lesser men known as the 'Cabal', and the development of a complicated political situation in which, as time went on, the King would play an increasingly important personal part, even as the opposition to his policies mounted. The effect on Charles II was marked. He still enjoyed life and maintained his happy demeanour; that was in his nature. But he was no longer the carefree libertine that he had been in the early years after his return to England. Life was now real and earnest to him. He became a wily statesman, playing off his opponents

The Great Fire of London, by Jan Wyck. With the double calamity of the Great Plague and the Great Fire, the bright dawn of the Restoration faded, and a new, graver era began.

Wren's Ideal City, from a drawing by Worthington G. Smith. Wren's 'glorious dream' might have made London 'one of Europe's most beautiful cities' but it would have cost too much to make it a reality.

against each other and taking public affairs more and more into his own hands. Ahead lay the ramifications of the Secret Treaty of Dover, the hysteria of the Popish Plot and the anti-monarchical plottings of the Exclusion Crisis. Always King Charles had one paramount aim—to protect the monarchy and consolidate his own control over the fortunes of his country. At length he succeeded; in the last few years of his life and reign he was the undisputed master of the nation, as near to being an absolute monarch as any of his predecessors.

The age that followed the Plague, the Fire and the Second Dutch War was more troubled and less light-hearted than that which preceded them. But the foundations built in 1660 remained firm. Republicanism had been defeated, and the English monarchy then re-established has, through various vicissitudes since then, stood the test of time. The building of a bigger and better London may be taken as symbolizing the triumph of the Restoration and the evolution of the modern age.

Bibliography

As this book is not based on original research, I have dispensed with footnotes and references. I have worked from printed authorities; books of which I have made most use are listed below.

ADLARD, JOHN, *The Fruit of that Forbidden Tree: Restoration Poems, Songs and Jests on the Subject of Sensual Love*, Fyfield Books, 1975.

ASHLEY, MAURICE, *Life in Stuart England*, Batsford, 1964.

Charles II: The Man and the Statesman, Weidenfeld & Nicolson, 1971.

General Monk, Jonathan Cape, 1977.

AUBREY, JOHN, *Brief Lives*, ed. A. Clark, Frowde, 1898.

BEDFORD, JOHN, *London's Burning*, Abelard-Schuman, 1966.

BELL, WALTER GEORGE, *The Great Fire of London in 1666*, Bodley Head, 1923.

The Great Plague in London in 1665, Bodley Head, 1924.

BRYANT, ARTHUR, *King Charles II*, Longman, 1931.

BURKE, THOMAS, *The Streets of London*, Batsford, 1940.

CHAPMAN, HESTER W., *The Tragedy of Charles II*, Jonathan Cape, 1964.

CHARLES II, KING, *Letters, Speeches and Proclamations*, ed. Arthur Bryant, Cassell, 1935.

CHILDS, JOHN, *The Army of Charles II*, Routledge & Kegan Paul, 1976.

CLARENDON, EDWARD EARL OF, *The History of the Rebellion and Civil Wars in England*, ed. W. Duncan Macray, Clarendon Press, 1888.

Continuation of Life, Clarendon Press, 1759.

CLARK, SIR GEORGE, *The Later Stuarts, 1660–1714*, Clarendon Press, 1955.

CLARK, PETER and SLACK, PAUL, *English Towns in Transition, 1500–1700*, Oxford University Press, 1976.

CLOWES, WILLIAM LAIRD, *The Royal Navy*, Low, 1897–1903.

COTTON, CHARLES, *The Compleat Gamester*, ed. Cyril Hughes Hartmann, Routledge & Kegan Paul, 1930.

CRAGG, G. R., *Puritanism in the Period of the Great Persecution, 1660–1688*, Cambridge University Press, 1957.

DUFFY, MAUREEN, *The Passionate Shepherdess: Aphra Behn, 1640–1689*, Jonathan Cape, 1977.

English Historical Documents, 1660–1714, ed. Andrew Browning, Eyre & Spottiswoode, 1953.

EVELYN, JOHN, *Diary,* ed. E. S. de Beer, Oxford University Press, 1955.

FORTESCUE, J. E., *History of the British Army,* Macmillan, 1899–1912.

FOSKETT, DAPHNE, *Samuel Cooper and his Contemporaries,* Faber & Faber, 1974.

GENEST, REV. JOHN, *Some Account of the English Stage,* Bath, 1832.'

GREENE, GRAHAM, *Lord Rochester's Monkey,* Hodder & Stoughton, 1974.

HAMILTON, ANTHONY, *Count Gramont at the Court of Charles II,* ed. and transl. Nicholas Deakin, Barrie & Rockcliff, 1965.

HOOK, JUDITH, *The Baroque Age in England,* Thames & Hudson, 1976.

JESSE, JOHN HENEAGE, *Memoirs of the Court of England,* Bentley, 1840.

KENYON, J. P., *The Stuart Constitution,* Cambridge University Press, 1966.

Stuart England, Allen Lane, 1978.

LEASOR, JAMES, *The Plague and the Fire,* Allen & Unwin, 1962.

LEWIS, MICHAEL, *The Navy of Britain,* Allen & Unwin, 1948.

Literary Anecdotes, the Oxford Book of, ed. James Sutherland, Clarendon Press, 1975.

MAHAN, CAPT. A. T., *The Influence of Sea Power upon History, 1660–1783,* Low, 1890.

MOLESWORTH, W. NASSAU, *History of the Church of England from 1660,* Routledge & Kegan Paul, 1882.

MORRAH, PATRICK, *1660: The Year of Restoration,* Chatto & Windus, 1960.

Prince Rupert of the Rhine, Constable, 1976.

PARTINGTON, J. R., *A History of Chemistry,* Macmillan, 1961.

PEPYS, SAMUEL, *The Diary of,* ed. Robert Latham and William Matthews, Bell, 1970–6.

PURVER, MARGERY, *The Royal Society: Concept and Creation,* Routledge & Kegan Paul, 1967.

RERESBY, SIR JOHN, *Memoirs of, 1634–89,* ed. J. J. Cartwright, Longman, 1875.

ROWSE, A. L., *Milton the Puritan,* Macmillan, 1977.

SORLEY, W. R., *A History of English Philosophy,* Cambridge University Press, 1937.

SUMMERSON, JOHN, *Architecture in Britain, 1530–1830,* Penguin, 1953.

TEDDER, ARTHUR W., *The Navy of the Restoration,* Cambridge University Press, 1919.

THORNBURY, WALTER, *Old and New London,* Low, 1873–78.

TREVELYAN, GEORGE MACAULAY, *England Under the Stuarts*, Methuen, 1904.

VERNEY, MARGARET M., *Memoirs of the Verney Family*, Longman, 1899.

WALKER, ERNEST, *A History of Music in England*, Clarendon Press, 1907.

WEDGWOOD, C. V., *Seventeenth-Century English Literature*, Oxford University Press, 1950.

WELD, CHARLES RICHARD, *A History of the Royal Society*, Parker, 1848.

WHINNEY, MARGARET and MILLAR, OLIVER, *English Art, 1625–1714*, Oxford University Press, 1957.

WILSON, JOHN HAROLD, *All the King's Ladies: Actresses of the Restoration*, Chicago, 1958.

Court Satires of the Restoration, Ohio State University Press, 1976.

WOOD, ANTHONY A., *Life and Times of*, ed. A. Clark, Oxford Historical Society, 1891–1900.

Index